MW00878479

"A WINNING BRAND"

"Separate yourself from your competition and create a personal brand that matters. Kraig Kleeman and his new book A Winning Brand will show you how."

- Brian Tracy,
Professional Speaker and Best Selling Author

"It's possible - and absolutely necessary - to create a thriving personal brand from scratch. Kraig Kleeman and A Winning Brand should be your guide to do just that."

- Max Altschuler,
CEO of SalesHacker

"If you have a burning desire to show the world your unique strengths, Kraig Kleeman's A Winning Brand is the handbook you've been looking for… and Kraig Kleeman is THE person you need to listen to."

- Gerhard Gschwandtner,
CEO, SellingPower

"The digital world has given you the power to create a thriving personal brand from scratch. Kraig Kleeman and A Winning Brand should be your road map to do just that."

- Stacy Tuschl,
Entrepreneur, #1 International Bestselling Author, Host of the top rated podcast on iTunes - She's Building Her Empire

"Your personal brand is the new resume. It's the new business card. It's the new currency. If you have massive goals, you need to brand yourself.

Kraig Kleeman is a master salesman who has taken a very deliberate, tactical approach to building his own brand and the brands of hundreds of individuals and companies.

A Winning Brand dives deep into the personal branding principles, strategies, social media tactics, and engagement techniques that will put you on the map.

Look, if you want to blow up your personal brand and make your name known, you have to listen to Kraig Kleeman. You have to read this book."

- Justin Gesso,
Bestselling Author
https://grindbehindbook.com

"Kraig Kleeman has already established himself as the king of personal branding. If you want to be known for what you do best, I highly recommend following Kraig's tips and tactics to build a winning brand. You won't regret it!"

- Karry Kleeman,
Chief Revenue Officer of SpringCM

"In the busy world we live in, it's more important than ever to create a brand that sets you apart from your competition. A Winning Brand is what every professional and entrepreneur needs."

- Randall LaVeau,
Marketing Practice Lead, Sales Benchmark Index

"In today's fast paced digital world developing your personal brand is equal to developing your professional brand. In many cases they will overlap.

Kraig's knowledge and insights help you navigate this landscape. Whether you are a seasoned professional or just getting started this book will provide you the right insights and exercises to make sure you are always on top of your game."

- Richard Harris,
The Harris Consulting Group

"You may miss the point when it comes to building your brand. You likely chase opportunities instead of attracting them, wander obscurely through the marketplace, and question why you've missed another sales target.

Kraig Kleeman wrote this book to shed light. He describes how to shape 'A Winning Brand' so you can level up your game and move the needle. If you don't yet believe in yourself, rest assured Kraig does. This book will pull you along a path that goes up and to the right."

- Ralph Barsi,
Leading Global Sales Development at ServiceNow

"Kraig Kleeman is a living legend in sales. Kraig's contribution to sales and sales development parallels greats like Zig Ziglar, Geoffrey Moore and Neil Rackham. In today's selling environment, it's imperative that you create a winning brand – Kraig will help you do just that!"

- Chad Burmeister,
Sr. Director, WW Sales Development, RingCentral

"I've known Kraig Kleeman for over 35 years and know that when you hear he is releasing a book, you sit up and listen. The man has influenced millions around the globe and now he's sharing how you can do the same by building your own brand."

- Dr. Kevin Noe

"A winning brand is essential for success in today's competition for attention. Learn the winning principals that the "World's Greatest Cold-Caller", Kraig Kleeman uses to differentiate, be unique, add-value and above all, be memorable."

- Danny Hughes,
Advisor, Author, Advocate, Social Entrepreneur

A WINNING BRAND

Kraig Kleeman

The World's Greatest Cold Caller
Kraigkleeman.com

Dedication

With a heart of joy I dedicate this book to my eldest son, Tyler Kleeman. With a lot of fatherly pride I have witnessed Tyler create a powerful, personal brand. He has developed a unique message and professional digital assets, along with consistency and boldness. He mentors young men in the Chicago community assisting them with a message of hope, restoration, and goodness.

I am confident that Tyler will continue his good work and I am very proud to be his father!

About
Kraig Kleeman

Kraig Kleeman is the World's Greatest Cold Caller. Kraig was founder and CEO of Express Direct, a technology company that sold digital pre-press solutions for high-end graphics designers. Kraig and his management team grew the company from $0-$25 million annual revenue in less than four years. During that rapid growth period, Kraig had responsibility for 25 professional sellers who completed more than one million sales presentations under his care. It was during this critical time of need to validate the plan and exceed corporate growth expectations that Kraig developed *The Must-React System*, the world's most predictable and efficient selling methodology.

After selling the company, Kraig took a few years off from the traditional work world by doing humanitarian outreach work in South America and Southeast Asia. At that time, he authored the book *The Must-React System*. Over the past seven years, Kraig has maintained a global sales transformation consulting practice. During his tenure as a Global Sales Strategist, Kraig has documented the findings of 25,000 distinct sales presentations across 46 different professional sales organizations. The results of Kraig's research are remarkable.

Kraig is recognized as the world's leading expert on sales process, sales transformation, and professional motivation. In the past 10 years, he has architected the entire selling model for more than 50 cloud-based computing companies, and more than 75 companies from other industries. From 2011-2014, sellers that were trained and certified in The Must-React System by Kraig Kleeman completed one million outreaches, scheduled 252,000 meetings (mostly with senior executives) and generated more than $400 million in net new revenue. He is founder of KraigKleemanTV, the world's most instructional sales training YouTube

Channel. Kraig is one of the most sought after speakers in the world.

Kraig has had the pleasure of speaking on panels / forums with President George W. Bush, British Prime Minister Tony Blair, Silicon Valley Guru Guy Kawasaki, and others.

Table of Contents

How To Read This Book

In today's crowded marketplace and job market, doing the norm is no longer good enough. It's more important than ever to understand how to position yourself – strategically and effectively – to stand apart. No matter what your role is, you have to stand for something. You have to have a brand.

This book will help you develop your own brand so that you stand apart from everyone else. In today's digital world, it is easier than ever for the average person to build an amazing brand to immunize themself against economic instability.

Success requires planning, boldness, hard work, and a willingness to fearlessly evaluate your talents and gifts. In this book, I help you do all of those things. I'll help you mine your talents and gifts and, along the way, help you discover strengths you never knew you had.

You can expect to closely examine your brand as it is now and discover how to get it to where you want it to be.

You'll learn about my journey before I guide you, step-by-step, through the process of creating your own winning brand.

Once you've finished reading the book, visit https://awinningbrand.com/ where you can see the details for my deep-dive course, **A Winning Brand by Kraig Kleeman**. This comprehensive course offers 20 step-by-step videos and 17 supplementary review guides to accompany this book. Together, they help clarify any questions you may have and give you even more in-depth guidance to building your winning brand.

Be bold, work hard, and be fearless in your quest to develop your brand.

Your friend and brand coach,

Kraig Kleeman

Introduction

As I write this, the parent company of Alaska Airlines is in the process of buying Virgin America for $2.6 billion. Shortly after the deal was announced, Virgin's famously devoted fans turned to social media to vent their concerns that the acquisition could result in the loss of what they loved about the airline – from its entertaining approach to its safety video to its well-heeled flight attendants to its on-board mood lighting.

"An iconic brand died today," wrote one Twitter user. Billionaire Richard Branson, who helped create the airline under the umbrella of his Virgin Group, responded to consumer concerns with a public letter in which he asserts, "The important thing now is to ensure that once Alaska witnesses first-hand the power of the brand and the love of Virgin America customers for our product and guest experience, they too will be converts."

What Richard Branson understands – and what makes the loyal customers of Virgin America so upset about the potential loss in an era when most airlines

Kraig Kleeman is The World's Greatest Cold Caller.

are regarded with apathy or even loathing – is the power of brand personality. In today's modern digital world, it is no longer enough to merely get the job done, or even to get it done well. Currently, there are more than 90 million Americans eligible for the work force who are un-

employed, and many more who are underemployed. You can no longer be a bureaucrat in a stereotypical operations, sales, or procurement role and survive in today's job market. In today's job market, you have to stand for something. **You have to have a brand.**

The world is getting more and more crowded, so it's more important than ever to understand how to strategically and effectively position yourself. This book will help you do just that. You have to assume that every person who interviews you, every person who takes a meeting with you – heck, even every person who goes on a date with you – has done a Google search for your name. As Branson himself has famously said, "In the beginning it was just about the business; now it's about the brand."

Luckily, in today's modern digital world, it is easier than ever before for the average person to build an amazing brand to immunize them against economic instability. In this book I will share with you my journey of building my own personal brand in this digital world, as well as guide you, step-by-step, through the process of creating your own winning brand.

My Personal Brand Journey

Some people work very hard,
but still they never get it right.
Well, I'm beginning to see the light.
Lou Reed, "Beginning to See the Light,"
The Velvet Underground (1972)

If you go to my LinkedIn page, or my Twitter feed, or my website kraigkleeman.com, you will see a polished, cohesive presentation of my personal brand. You'll see

"I decided to reinvent myself and dive into the modern digital age."

photos of me in my usual dark glasses and peace sign necklaces. You'll see inspirational messages. You'll see references to my reputation as "The World's Greatest

Cold Caller." But I haven't always had this comprehensive, meaningful brand strategy. Just a few short years ago, I had no personal brand. I had a strong work ethic and a solid set of skills and talents that had helped me succeed in my sales and consulting careers. I had almost no involvement in social media and I had not yet "seen the light," in terms of how to leverage it in order to increase my influence. At that time in my life, I was also undergoing a serious health crisis and finding my way through a period of emotional turmoil in my familial and personal relationships. As a response to this instability in my life, I decided to reinvent myself and dive into the modern digital age. Doing so required me to undertake a serious process of self-examination. I read somewhere that self-deception is the worst form of deception. I like to say, "Self-examination is the best form of examination."

This process of reinvention taught me a lot. I learned that you don't need a lot of money in order to take charge of your personal brand journey – all you need is a computer, a smart phone, and access to the Internet. On a more philosophical level, I also learned that you are not defined by your circumstances. In the words of Scott Bedbury, the former advertising director of Nike who helped launch the "Just Do It" campaign, "A great brand is a story that's never completely told… stories create the emotional context people need to locate themselves in a larger experience." In my personal story, I decided that I wanted something more than a career in middle management. I wanted to impact people on a large scale, to help people do their jobs better, to teach them how to create success. To do that, I had to be willing to expand my story about who I was. Like me, you have control over crafting your story, over defining yourself for the world. And that story is, and must be, ongoing. Every new YouTube video you make, every new link you post on Facebook, and every new Tweet is a new page in your story. That story – that winning brand – is what will enable you to create both wealth and influence.

If you have read my book The Must-React System, then you already know how I developed my natural gift for persuasion into a winning methodology for sales teams. My transition from talented sales associate to world-renowned consultant didn't happen overnight. It's one thing to be a natural born cold caller. It's quite another to become known as "the world's greatest cold caller." The difference is branding. In order to increase my success in management consulting, I first had to develop a sales strategy that was reproducible. Further, I gave that strategy a memorable name that captured the essential tenets of the method – "The Must-React System."

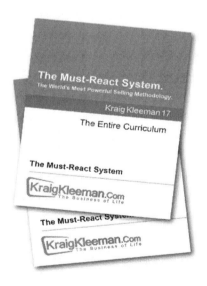

"This period was a pivotal point in my personal brand journey."

As my clients began to have success with my system, my consulting referrals increased, and clients gave me the nickname "the world's greatest cold caller." This period was a pivotal point in my personal brand journey. Not only was my reach already increasing as a result of the system itself, but this new nickname paved the way for my influence to increase exponentially further. I already thought "the world's greatest cold caller" was a good way to distinguish myself, but once I did some online research and discovered how incredibly often the term "cold calling" is searched, I knew for sure that adopting that moniker would have a profound impact on my brand.

Along with customizing my digital domain and being known as "the world's greatest cold caller," here are a few other pivotal moments or factors that were key in boosting my brand:

1. My book managed to get into the hands of the right people, and word about my system started to spread. Having influential people advocate for your work is priceless.

> **Two major steps in my personal brand journey:**
>
> **Step 1:** Secure and customize my official digital domain, kraigkleeman.com
> **Step 2:** Adopt and leverage the moniker of "the world's greatest cold caller"

2. As the people who have worked with me or read my first book know, I owe part of my brand journey to an encounter with Bono. While on vacation in Amsterdam, I saw him sitting alone in a bar, and was able to gain an unsolicited 45-minute meeting with him by appealing to his core values of "defending the poor of the earth." When I first started retelling that story to clients, it served to illustrate the importance of finding out what matters to your sales prospects. It still serves that purpose quite well. But as time has passed, the story has also become part of the bigger story of my brand. The anecdote appears in my first book, on my website, and on my LinkedIn page. I have become known as the guy who landed the impromptu meeting with one of the greatest rock performers in history. In fact, Bono, himself, wrote the foreword to The Must-React System.

3. In a similar way that Bono lends celebrity appeal to my brand, my personal appearances at high-profile events such as ringing the NASDAQ bell and sharing a stage with George W.

Bush and Tony Blair, have increased my visibility and influence.

Kraig delivers keynote address at the Nasdaq Tower, Times Square

4. I have been fortunate to connect with the right people in the tech community, such as when I was discovered by Ken Krogue, the founder of Insidesales.com, who helped me get invitations to speak on panels with other influential people, and then co-authored an e-book with me.

5. Whether I am giving a keynote speech at a conference, or working with clients one on one, I have found a way to always be myself in my professional life. For example, I love classic rock n' roll. I always have. I also believe that rock lyrics are a great way to con-

nect to people because they are familiar, they resonate, and they provide common ground. For these reasons, you'll find rock lyrics peppered throughout my talks, videos, and written work. I'm also known for wearing peace sign necklaces. I wear them because I believe in the importance of peace, both globally and individually. Perhaps my most recognizable trait, though, is that I always wear sunglasses. People always ask me about them. I do love sunglasses; I own more than 300 pairs! But they are more to me than just a fashion accessory; they remind me of the power of perspective and the importance of keeping a fresh point of view. So they, too, are part of my brand – sure, they do make me consistently recognizable, but, more importantly, they reinforce key principles I believe in.

6. Going to video – Rod Stewart says that "Every picture tells a story." I say, "Every video tells a thousand stories." It's important to make yourself visible to your audience, and video is a great way to keep your brand journey moving forward. If you make a memorable video, your whole audience will want to connect with you.

As a result of leveraging the assets of the digital age to my advantage, I was able to create both personal wealth and global influence. My name is known globally because of my areas of expertise: cold calling, sales process performance, and persuasion in the realm of business. Ever since I rebranded for the digital world, my personal brand has grown exponentially:

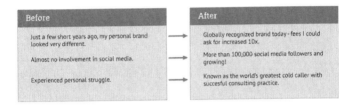

My purpose in sharing my story is not to puff myself up, but for you to see that small opportunities can give rise to bigger opportunities, and that the more you put yourself out there, the more momentum you build. My success certainly didn't happen overnight. Success requires planning, boldness, hard work, and a willingness to fearlessly evaluate your talents and gifts. Sure, I didn't plan to run into Bono that night in Amsterdam, but if I hadn't had the boldness to put myself out there and approach him, nor the follow-through to apply that experience to my brand-building journey, I might not be where I am today. My book and course materials are here to help you achieve that same kind of momentum.

ACTION STEPS

Now, it's your turn to think about your own winning brand. Take a few minutes to answer the following questions:

- What does your personal brand look like right now?

- What do you want your brand to become?

Building Your Own Winning Brand

And you give yourself away
And you give yourself away
And you give
And you give
And you give yourself away
- U2, "With or Without You," The Joshua Tree (1987)

The same process that has made my name a global brand can help you build your own winning brand. You just have to be willing to give yourself away completely to the digital age and all the opportunities that come with it. Sometimes we may think that the phrasing "give yourself away" can have negative connotations, as in giving away part of our identity or overextending ourselves by giving too much to others, but that's not what I mean here. In terms of your personal brand, giving yourself away means to get your name out there, to circulate your brand, to build recognition, to get in front of as many eyes as possible. So I'd encourage you to give yourself away at every relevant opportunity – give yourself away on your website, on LinkedIn, on Facebook, on Twitter, on Instagram. Don't think for a minute that you'll be losing something through all this giving. Quite the contrary! As I mentioned, once I started crafting my image by customizing my digital domain, I was able to charge a 10x premium for my consulting services.

You need to stay current and keep your brand fresh in people's minds. If people don't remember you, then potential clients, customers, and connections won't know to contact you.

In this book you will learn about three key components that have led me to where I am today on my brand journey, components that you can follow to craft your own winning image in the digital landscape:

Winning Brand Principles:

These five principles, which I will explain in more depth in the next section, are:
- Attitude – Be Bold. Embrace External Perspective. Remain Intellectually Curious.
- Take Inventory – Discover your winning brand mix by taking inventory of your skills, talents, and abilities.
- Discover Originality – Think about what sets your brand apart from all of the others. What is your personal brand identifier?
- Be Consistent – It is essential to communicate a consistent message. Make sure your originality is consistent with your brand.
- Get Visible – Expand your visibility through digital platforms.

> **Three key tools to lead you to success:**
>
> See your personal brand benefit by leveraging the following:
> - Principles — Five principles that are philosophical in nature.
> - Steps — Three major steps with several sub-steps.
> - Effectiveness Tracking — Monitoring success and tangible growth.

And then last but certainly not least, you will need to track your efforts. You need to see what types of efforts yield the biggest payoff. Monitoring your results, for example, will give you important information about what media channels you should be spending more time on, which time of day you should be posting content in order to get the largest viewership, and what groups of followers are most active and influential, in terms of their engagement.

> **Three major steps:**
>
> We will also explore three major concrete steps, each of which has several sub-steps. These steps are:
> - Step 1 — Craft your image
> - Step 2 — Develop your story
> - Step 3 — Take your brand digital

In the coming chapters, I will guide you through leveraging all of these components in order to build a brand that is **bold**, **memorable**, and **influential**.

ACTION STEPS

Looking back on the information in this chapter, par-
ticularly the key tools that will lead to success, the
Winning Brand Principles, and the major steps, it's
your turn to start your own branding journey. Identify
the resources that you know you will need to build
your own bold, memorable brand. Open up your
mind; don't discount something because you feel it is
out of reach.

Brainstorm: What resources will you need to build a bold and memorable brand?

Winning Brand Principles

I'm free to sing my song though it gets out of time
I'm free to sing my song though it gets out of time
So love me, hold me, hold me, love me
And I'm free to do what I want any old time.
Mick Jagger and Keith Richards, "I'm Free"
– The Rolling Stones,
Out of Our Heads (1965)

I owe all of my current success to my willingness to dive into the digital age and to use its assets to craft and broadcast my winning brand. Here are the five fundamental principles that will guide you on your own personal brand journey.

Principle 1: Attitude

Be Bold, Embrace External Perspectives, Remain Intellectually Curious

Being bold is important. Don't be shy about building your brand. Remember, I'm the guy who adopted the distinction of "the world's greatest cold caller"! You shouldn't be shy about putting yourself out there in the digital world, and frankly you can't afford to be. You need to be your own strongest advocate. Be dauntlessly brave.

"You never know where a great idea might come from."

In addition to being bold, open yourself up to embrace the power of external perspectives. The business world sometimes has a tendency to idolize the figure of the individual genius – e.g., Andrew Carnegie, Ted Turner, or Steve Jobs. But successful business leaders, including Steve Jobs, have recognized the importance of outside perspectives. Jobs himself has said, "Innovation comes from people meeting up in the hallways or calling each other at 10:30 at night with a new idea, or because they realized something that shoots holes in how we've been thinking about a problem. It's ad hoc meetings of six people called by someone who thinks he has figured out the coolest new thing ever and who wants to know what other people think of his idea." In fact, he asserted that the insularity of the tech industry often holds back creativity and inventiveness: "A lot of people in our industry haven't had very diverse experiences. So they don't have enough dots to connect, and they end up with very linear solutions without a broad perspective on the problem. The broader one's understanding of the human experience, the better design we will have." Without external perspectives, organizations and individuals stagnate and innovation can't thrive. Further, it is important to stay open to new information and remain teachable. In order to make an impact in your field, you have to know what the relevant topics, ideas, advances, and conversations are. Be willing to consider input or even critiques from friends, colleagues, and mentors. Doing so may help you avoid making mistakes, or it may help you find ways to remedy mistakes you've already made.

Closely related to this idea of embracing outside perspectives is the concept of remaining teachable and exercising your intellectual curiosity. You never know where a great idea might come from. Your brand journey will likely require you to learn about new technology platforms, meet new people, and put yourself in unfamiliar situations. These experiences may sometimes be uncomfortable, but in every instance, ask yourself what you can learn and how this new knowledge can better enable you to tell your story. Approaching every new step in your journey with what's called a "beginner's mindset" will be a huge benefit to you in building your brand. Technology is constantly evolving, and so must our skill sets.

How open and teachable are you?

Rate yourself on the questions below on a scale of 1-5:

(1 = Never, 2 = Hardly Ever, 3 = Sometimes, 4 = Most of the Time, 5 = Always)

I am willing to put myself in unfamiliar situations in order to grow.

1   2   3   4   5

When I am in an unfamiliar situation, I look for what's positive and try to keep an open mind.

1   2   3   4   5

When I receive criticism, I think about the feedback I have received before I react.

1   2   3   4   5

When I fail at something, I look for the lessons I can learn to improve my performance in the future.

1   2   3   4   5

When someone presents me with a convincing argument that counters my own viewpoint, I am willing to revise that viewpoint.

1   2   3   4   5

I seek trusted feedback on projects before completing them/turning them in.

1   2   3   4   5

Now add up your score. The higher it is, the more teachable you tend to be. A score of 32-40 means you are highly open and teachable. The good news is, opening yourself up is something we choose to do, and something you can get better at with practice and awareness.

Principle 2: Take Inventory

Discover your winning gift mix.

We all have gifts, and we all have limitations. As I mentioned earlier, an essential ingredient of my gift mix is my skill as a cold caller: I can get a meeting with practically anyone, from C-suite executives to celebrities. It's something I've known I was good at since I was a teenager in St. Louis talking my way onto the air every weekend on my favorite radio show. A few years down the road, I impressed my college professors by landing an in-person lunch meeting with the Reverend Jesse Jackson when some fellow students and I went to Chicago. These skills have been the foundation of my success in sales, consulting, and now in building my brand.

For the infamous hacker-turned-security-consultant Kevin Mitnick, the key to success is his ability to infiltrate computer networks. His talent, because he initially exercised it outside the limits of the law, landed him in prison for five years, but he was nevertheless able to rebuild his professional life through using that same talent. He has always maintained that, for him, the goal of hacking was never to profit financially, but to follow his passion: "It was about intellectual curiosity and pursuit of knowledge and the thrill." Now, he uses his gifts to help governments and leading corporations test their security. And he markets himself as "the world's most famous hacker." He found a way to reframe a low point in his life – i.e., his arrest and prison sentence – as a defining pivot point for his brand by drawing on his unique talents.

Taking inventory will help you discover your own gift mix, and there is an exercise at the end of this chapter to help you do just that. Get connected with how you are hardwired as a person. Think about what talents you have that you can leverage to create your winning brand. What expertise do people seek you out for?

What do people tend to expect from you when they hire you or ask for your input? What activities make you feel confident when you engage in them? What abilities reliably yield positive results for you? Self-reflection is an important part of taking inventory, but don't forget to embrace the power of outside perspectives and ask your friends, family, and coworkers what they think your strengths are.

Principle 3: Discover Originality

Find something that identifies your brand.

When we think about memorable individuals, we typically think of them in terms of what distinguishes them from the crowd. Johnny Cash, for example, was known for wearing black in an era when country singers wore flamboyant sequined suits and cowboy boots. At a time when most TV hosts were white men, Oprah Winfrey persevered in her quest to establish a media career, and she set herself apart with an emotional authenticity that viewers found appealing. As I mentioned in the introductory chapter, for me the "something" that identifies my brand is my classic rock 'n roll vibe: my mental filing cabinet full of song lyrics, my sunglasses, the peace signs I wear. Obviously I'm not suggesting that you should wear sunglasses and peace signs every day, but you **should** find what it is that can help you distinguish your personal brand.

Did you ever try to pretend that you liked something you didn't, or to try to be someone you weren't, in order to fit in with a peer group, escape criticism, or avoid family conflict? It's exhausting isn't it? Can you imagine doing that all the time? Building your brand will be much easier if you evaluate who you are and remain true to that vision, rather than trying to contort yourself in an attempt to please everyone. Chances are, it wouldn't work anyway.

People can sense authenticity, and they can sense its lack as well. Part of being bold is embracing your individuality. Your brand is a promise you have to be able to live up to.

Principle 4: Be Consistent

Make sure the originality is consistent with what your brand is intending to communicate.

Once you decide what defines your personal brand, make sure that you cultivate an image that is consistent with those traits. By being consistent, you establish and maintain credibility. If something doesn't match the message you are trying to convey, then don't do it, say it, wear it, or post it. Be strategic and purposeful about what you do, say, wear, and post. For example, since Derek Jeter retired from baseball, he has focused much of his energy on his charity organization, Turn 2 Foundation, the purpose of which is to promote to healthy lifestyles among young people by helping them avoid drug and alcohol addiction. These days, his social media channels are filled with stories related to motivation, health, the organization itself, and, of course, baseball. What you **don't** see are images of Jeter partying or holding an alcoholic drink. If you did see that, it would damage Jeter's credibility as a spokesman for his organization.

To quote Steve Jobs, "People think focus means saying yes to the thing you've got to focus on. But that's not what it means at all. It means saying no to the hundred other good ideas that there are. You have to

*Steven Jobs taught us the impor-
tance of external perspectives.*

pick carefully. I'm actually as proud of the things we haven't done as the things I have done."

Read through the following list, and think about what the following aspects of your life might tell you about your individual traits, and how those traits might be applied to your personal brand:

- The way you write emails
- Your personal grooming and style habits
- The music you prefer to listen to
- Objects you collect
- Games, sports, or hobbies you enjoy
- The types of posts you make on social media
- Your engagement with a church, social club, charity, or other community organization
- The way you conduct yourself in meetings
- The way you introduce yourself to new people
- The type of setting that recharges and energizes you
- Your ideal client or ideal manager, if you could design one

Do you notice any common threads as you evaluate these aspects of your life and personality? If so, what are they?

Principle 5: Get Visible

Expand your personal brand's reach digitally.

The steps in this book are designed to help you become visible across multiple digital platforms, including Facebook, LinkedIn, Twitter, Instagram, and YouTube. What social platforms do you use now? What platforms do you hope to expand to?

> So, how can you apply these 5 principles? You can start with the following exercise, which guides you through a **Personal Brand Inventory**.

ACTION STEPS

In this chapter, I told you about five Winning Brand principles. I focused on attitude and how teachable you are, discovering your winning gifts and originality, the importance of being consistent, and of being visible. For the next step in your journey to developing a Winning Brand, honestly answer the questions in the Personal Brand Inventory, below. Then, conduct a personal reflection to evaluate your own winning gifts.

Personal Brand Inventory

Current

- **Values:** What one to two personal beliefs influence your choices and actions?
- **Interests & Passions:** What issues, causes, activities, or hobbies are you passionate about?
- **Mission:** What are you committed to accomplishing, in the short-term or long-term?
- **Vision:** How do you see yourself using your mission?
- **Stregths:** What positive assets have brought you positive outcomes? What are others complimenting you on?
- **One-In-A-Million:** What makes you different from everyone else? Describe the unique quality that makes you, YOU!
- **Reflection:** How do others describe you?

Future

- **Best in Class:** If you could be the best in the world at one thing...
  - Look at the values you evaluated above (Current). How do you wish to be known? Select one to get started. (Ex: Sense of humor; Organization)
  - Do you need to learn any additional skills?
  - Do you know people who can help you with this role?
- **Personal slogan:** Use www.slogangenerator.org/ to generate your own personal slogan. Remember to use your name and include your best in class strength.
  - How will you embrace a winning attitude?
  - What is your WINNING BRAND mix?

Your Turn

- Complete the Personal Brand Reflection found on the following page.
- Take inventory of your accomplishments and personal gift-mix to generate a bold and memorable tagline.

Critically Evaluate Your Personal Gift Mix

Personal Reflection	
Review your own talents and critically evaluate what makes your brand bold.	
Question:	**Your Reflection:**
Describe your personal brand as it stands today.	
What gifts do you possess that others have recognized? (Think: What typically sets you apart from the others?)	
What are your talents? (1-2)	
Consistent with your skills/talents, what would you like to be known for?	
How can you communicate (what you want to be known for) in a bold and powerful way? What research will you do?	
What taglines can you use to boost persuasive impact of your personal gift-mix?	

Your Digital Dot Com

Come here mama, and dig this crazy scene
He's not too fancy, but his mind is pretty clean
He ain't no drag
Papa's got a brand new bag
James Brown, "Papa's Got a Brand New Bag" (1965)

The next sections of the book will walk you through how to craft your image by customizing your domain for personal branding. As the world becomes more and more dependent on the digital realm for business transactions, referrals, and community interactions, we have to learn to leverage the opportunities of that realm, or else we will be left behind. An article in Forbes in 2013 cited a study by Workfolio, a company that develops applications to help people enhance their online visibility, which found that "Fifty-six percent of all hiring managers are more impressed by a candidate's personal website than any other personal branding tool—however, only 7% of job seekers actually have a personal website." What a wasted opportunity! Rather than let the digital age pass us by, out of apathy or intimidation, we should be like the old man in James Brown's famous song "Papa's Got a Brand New Bag:" enthusiastic about learning new moves and showing them off! Whether you are a job seeker or an entrepreneur, you'll want to make your brand as visible as possible.

KraigKleeman.com branded domain

As we have seen, my own business grew by leaps and bounds once I established an official "kraigklee-man.com" website and incorporated my tagline of "The World's Greatest Cold Caller" into the rhetoric of the site. Once I had a website, I had a primary online avenue for announcing new initiatives and creating the story of my winning brand, and I had a place to consolidate assets, from my contact information, to client testimonials, to links that could take visitors to my blog or to my YouTube videos.

As a result of the success of my domain:

- I was able to command 10x more for my consulting services than I had previously charged.
- My business referrals and the demand for my services increased.
- I began to receive regular invitations to speak ar star-studded events.
- I was invited to speak at online webcast events, increasing my digital reach even further!

In order to build your own winning brand, it is essential to **fully commit** to taking that brand digital. Keep that attitude of boldness, openness, and intellectual curiosity, and you will be ready to receive all the goodness that comes with giving yourself completely to the digital world!

Your website will:

- Establish you as a thought leader in the areas of expertise around which you will build your brand.
- Work as an enhanced version of a resume that lets people know about your skills, experiences, talents, values, passions, etc.
- Announce your digital reputation.

In addition to fulfilling these purposes, digital branding is also a cost effective way to reach your target audiences or market demographics. Building your website could be the most important step in creating your own digital brand.

ACTION STEPS

Now it's time to build your online presence, starting with your domain and tagline. This is the first thing people will discover about you or look for, so it's important to take the time to come up with something that is memorable and descriptive of your brand.

Personal Reflection Answer the questions below to evaluate your winning gift-mix to generate a memorable tagline.	
Question:	**Your Reflection:**
What website domain name will be easy for clients to search? *(Note: FirstLastname.com is recommended but not always available)*	
How do your colleagues, clients and coworkers say your work is different from everybody else's?	
How would you describe yourself in 2-3 words?	
Use this website to help you determine your own slogan or moniker (if you do not have one already): http://www.slogangenerator.org/	

Securing Your Domain

Ultimately, securing your domain is a two-step process, and it doesn't really matter which of the two comes first. We will be using GoDaddy.com to get our branded website online, and Branded.me to build our website. Completing these two steps is how you plant your first flag in the digital landscape.

Format suggestion:
firstnamelastname.com
ex: kraigkleeman.com

One thing to remember: I highly recommend
using the "firstnamelastname.com" naming convention
for your site. It's simple, and it's easy for your connections
and clients to remember.

Step 1: Find a host for your branded website (GoDaddy.com)

A host is a company that houses, serves, and maintains files for one or more websites. GoDaddy is a host, a third-party website that helps you get online. It costs just a few dollars to host and maintain your site.

Step 2: Build your branded website (Branded.me in course 6)

Go to branded. me to get started.

You can't have a website without a domain — that is why it is important that we have a well-branded domain that communicates our personal brand. We will need the custom domain because we will be connecting the domain with the Limited or PRO version of Branded.me. Your domain name is what people type into their browser to find your site.

ACTION STEPS

To Begin Hosting Your Site With GoDaddy, Follow These Steps

Step 1: Go to GoDaddy.com
- Type www.godaddy.com into your browser.
- In the search bar, type the domain to check availability.
- Click Search Domain button.

Step 2: Select a Domain Option
- GoDaddy.com will offer a list of alternative domain name(s) if your domain is not available. Select from the list by scrolling.
- *Note: Annual price for each domain namelisted in orange.*
- Click the green Select button to own the domain and continue.

Step 3: Evaluate & Continue to Purchase
- Think about it...
  - Does the selected domain align with your personal brand?
  - Will others associate the domain with your personal brand?
  - How will this domain name help your brand?
- If (and when) you feel confident about your answers, select the orange Continue to Cart button in the upper left-hand corner.

Step 4: Proceed to Checkout
- GoDaddy.com will ask you to purchase several "add-ons," simply continue to purchase.
- Create a GoDaddy.com account to complete your purchase.
- Make sure to remember your GoDaddy.com account information!
- Congrats! You own your own domain!

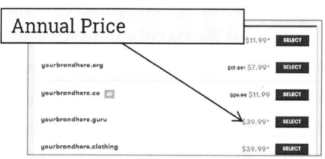

Annual Price

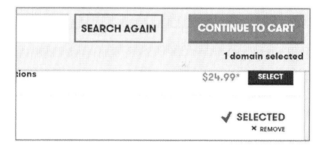

> Reflect on your digital domain here:
>
> ....
> ....
> ....
> ....
> ....

After signing up for your digital dot com, you have successfully established your digital domain! Now it's time to add your personal branded content.

ACTION STEPS

To Begin Using Branded. Me, Follow These Steps

Step 1: Go to Branded.me
- Type www.branded.me into your browser.
- On the right-hand side of your screen, hover over the blue button Sign Up Now For Free
- Click a sign-up option. (NOTE: We will be using email.) Enter your email information.

Step 2: Confirm & Complete
- You will receive a confirmation email. Go to your inbox and confirm by selecting the url.
- Complete your account information, including your First Name, Last Name and Password.
- Click Create Account.

Step 3: Select Your Network
- Branded.me recommends following 20 people to get started. If you see a green checkmark in the upper left-hand corner, the person WILL be added when you continue.
- To remove all, click "Unselect All" on the bottom of your screen.
- To remove individual people, click individual checkmarks.
- Click Follow & Continue button on bottom right.

Step 4: Design Your Digital Personal Brand
- To get started, select the Design tab along on the top.
  - – Design Menu: On the left-hand side, controls the style of your page.
  - – Content Menu: On the top, controls the readable content viewers will see.

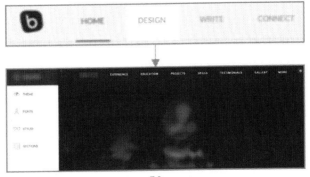

Once you start uploading your content, the new you will be announced!

Kraig's personal friend and mentor, U2's Bono.

After you complete these two simple but crucial steps, you are well on your way to building and proning brand. Once make it a habit to search your domain name on Google in order to see how you are being perceived, and if that perception is consistent with the brand you're building. The online realm is constantly evolving, so be prepared to add to, subtract from, and tweak your site throughout your brand journey. Remember those Bono lyrics I mentioned earlier in the book – **"And you give, and you give, and you give yourself away."** Now that you made your commitment to your digital brand, you will be able to give yourself away at levels you could not previously have imagined! Increased referrals, increased visibility, increased credibility: all of these benefits arise as a result of the exposure that is available only through digital platforms.

What Makes Your Brand Bold?

Now each of us has his own special gift
And you know this was meant to be true
And if you don't underestimate me
I won't underestimate you.
Bob Dylan, "Dear Landlord"- John Wesley Harding (1967)

Throughout history people of influence have recognized the importance of self-knowledge. Socrates famously said, *"Know thyself."* Ben Franklin said, *"Observe all men; thy self most."* More recently, legendary tennis pro Billie Jean King said, *"I think self-awareness is probably the most important thing towards being a champion."* In this chapter I will challenge you to critically evaluate yourself so that you understand what makes your brand bold. At the end of the chapter, you will take a personal inventory that will help you critically evaluate your personal "gift mix" and accomplishments and come up with your own bold, memorable taglines. With the insights you get from this inventory exercise, you can start building a brand that others will see in an optimal light.

Kevin Plank, the founder and CEO of the disruptive athletic apparel company Under Armour, understands the importance of figuring out what you do well. In an article on Inc.com, Plank says, *"For the first five years, as we grew our company from zero to $5 million, we made, really, one shirt. Another way to say it is that a company needs to become famous for something, to find that niche. In those early years, we didn't try to keep up with the Joneses and make 10 other styles and different things; we created one thing."* When the time came to expand into other product areas, Plank made sure to stay true to the principles that people associated with Under Armour: *"I realized that it was not just this product I was building; it was a brand. Under Armour wasn't about the compression T-shirt; it was about the essence of it: performance."* And Under Armour has stayed true to that vision – that tagline, if you will – of performance. The company has certainly expanded its offerings, but has kept its focus in the product areas where its brand strengths lie (e.g., sporting apparel, athletic shoes, and sporting accessories), and its vision statement lines up with that: **"Empower athletes everywhere."**

I owned my management consulting practice for quite some time before I figured out how to make my brand a truly bold one. In my role as a consultant, I helped companies establish better sales processes and sometimes even stimulated complete sales process transformation. As I have mentioned, I have a natural gift for persuasion and for getting people on the phone, and I used that gift to help my clients improve the success of their sales teams' outreach efforts. As a result of the great outcomes they had with the practices I pioneered, my clients affectionately gave me the nickname, "The World's Greatest Cold Caller." I was flattered and humbled, and I decided that if people widely recognized my cold calling skill as an essential component of my personal gift mix, then it would be a smart move for me to make it part of my brand. I did some research and found that "cold calling" is a widely searched term on the internet. I met with advisors, did some split A/B testing, and came to the conclusion that this nickname would indeed have a positive impact on my brand.

In addition to adopting the nickname, I decided to change how I talked about the successful sales process that I had developed. It wouldn't have been enough to just talk about "Kraig Kleeman's Advice" or "Assistance from Some Consultant Named Kraig Kleeman" - those phrases aren't memorable. Instead, I decided to call it "The Must-React System." Even though each individual engagement was customized for a particular client, this bold, impactful name succinctly captures the main tenets of the system.

Kraig leads a Must-React Workshop onsite at a client location.

Once I had the name, I started using it everywhere! And inquiries for my services really took off. Honestly, I could not have predicted the great impact that the taglines "The World's Greatest Cold Caller" and "The Inventor of the Must-React System" would have. And the opportunities that arose as a result of the success of **those** two pivotal moments paved the way for further professional growth, which led to me being able to adopt additional taglines. For example, "The King of Personal Branding" has become a new tagline for me, as a result of my recent work with branding.

To sum up, the steps I followed in my own brand journey —

Follow these recommended steps to define your winning brand:
- **Build branded sustainable systems that are repeatable.** Use the branded name EVERYWHERE. Make sure the name describes the system.
- **Do your research.** Run A/B tests, look at the most searched terms associated with your personal gift-mix, talk to trusted advisors. Decide what personal moniker will have a positive impact on your personal brand.

ACTION STEPS

Now that you've learned the importance of being bold in your brand, build your own bold story. Focus on your Winning Brand tagline, system, and plan.

Your personal brand journey:

Your tagline ....
....
....
....

Your system ....
....
....
....

Your plan ....
....
....
....

Personal Brand Reflection

*"Self-awareness gives you the capacity to learn from
your mistakes as well as your successes.
It enables you to keep growing."*
– Larry Bossidy, author and retired CEO of Honeywell

Now it's your turn. The point of the following exercise is to give you more clarity around what makes you unique. Getting that clarity requires honesty from you and from the people you ask to fill out your questionnaire. Begin by asking yourself the following questions:

Personal Reflection	
Review your own talents and critically evaluate what makes your brand bold.	
Question:	**Your Reflection:**
How would you describe your personal brand today?	
What gifts do you possess that others have recognized? (Think: What typically sets you apart from the others?)	
What are your talents? (1-2)	
Consistent with your skills/talents, what would you like to be known for?	
How can you communicate (what you want to be known for) in a bold and powerful way? What research will you do?	
What taglines can you use to boost persuasive impact of your personal gift-mix?	

I cannot stress enough that honesty is crucial to this process. When you build a brand, you are setting a standard for yourself and your audience or clients that you need to be able to live up to. So it is absolutely essential that you get real about what you're good at, not what you **wish** you were good at. If you stay true to yourself, maintaining your brand will feel authentic to both you and your target audience. It will also make your efforts more sustainable and consistent in the long run.

Talents come in many forms: For example, are you driven and aggressive? Or more laid back and approachable? Do people seek you out because you excel at delivering results quickly? Or, conversely, because you specialize in long-term relationship building? Are you good at working with numbers? Or maybe working with your hands? Are you creative? If so, in what way? Are you a creative problem solver, or do you have a creative flair for visual design, or are you a gifted storyteller? Are you good at organization? If so, how? Are you good at organizing spaces? Events? People? Are you good at leading or influencing others, or do you find that you perform better when you are supporting a team?

As you reflect on your gifts and accomplishments, send the following survey to your clients (Remember what I said earlier about staying open to outside perspectives?). Compare the answers with how you perceive your own personal brand. Once you compile the results and compare them with your own, you can develop at least one tagline – preferably two or three – that is bold and memorable.

Send this personal gift mix survey to clients.

Adopt A Winning Facebook Strategy

For though they may be parted
There is still a chance that they will see
There will be an answer, let it be
Yeah, let it be, let it be, let it be, let it be
There will be an answer, let it be.
The Beatles, "Let It Be" – Paul McCartney

Every day social media is becoming more and more entrenched in our daily lives. One of the great benefits of social media channels is the way they bring people together. We use social media to keep in touch with distant family and friends, to let others know where we are and what we're doing (and even what we're eating), to announce big life changes, and to plan social events. These social media platforms are fantastic tools for anyone building a brand because they are freely available, and they have millions upon millions of subscribers. These platforms make it easier than ever for you to share your personal brand with the world.

Facebook is, by far, the largest and most active of these social media platforms. In the spring of 2016, Techcrunch reported that Facebook currently has 1.65 billion users around the world. According to Facebook's recent numbers, 1.09 billion of those subscribers log on daily (DAU, or Daily Active Users). We all sometimes use Facebook as a way to communicate with others one-on-one through messaging and commenting. But, of course, it is also enables us to share images and videos and statements publicly, and with 1.65 billion users, just imagine the potential for expanding the reach of your brand! Facebook founder and CEO Mark Zuckerberg has said, "Think about what people are doing on Facebook today. They're keeping up with their friends and family, but they're also building an image and identity for themselves, which in a sense is their brand. They're connecting with the audience that they want to connect to. It's almost a disadvantage if you're not on it now." I would go one step further and say that "almost" stops short of the truth; it **absolutely is** a disadvantage if you're not on it now.

If you need any convincing (although I doubt you do), consider the following statistics: According to the Salesforce State of Marketing report in 2015, Facebook is the number one social media channel for marketers, and eighty percent of marketers use it. A survey featured by Search Engine Journal reveals that forty-six percent of Americans identify Facebook as their top influencer of purchases, up from twenty-four percent in 2011. Mark Zuckerberg recently stated that the average time that users spend on Facebook's combined platforms of Facebook, Messenger, and Instagram has climbed to fifty minutes per day. Those fifty minutes account for about twenty percent of the total time spent on mobile devices. The famous action-movie actor Vin Diesel once made the humorous observation that "If Clark Gable had a Facebook page, there would have been a *Gone with the Wind 2*." Looking at these numbers, I can't help but think that he's right.

What I want you to do is start thinking about Facebook as a strategic tool for building your brand. If you haven't signed up for Facebook yet, or if your participation has been pretty passive up to this point, don't worry - you can start your strategic approach now. A few short years ago, when I first signed up for Facebook, initially I wasn't that engaged with it. I posted mundane status updates without putting much thought into them, or pictures of my daily activities, like a lot of people do. And, like most people, I'm sure I was guilty of posting pictures of fairly unre-markable dinners at some point.

"Start thinking about Facebook as a strategic tool
for building your brand."

But once I started thinking of Facebook as a strategic asset, I realized that I needed to change that approach. I didn't want to post pictures that looked like just anyone could have taken them. Instead, I needed to post content that reflected the personal brand I was building.

One pivotal moment that drove this home for me was an occasion when I was working and posted a line from "Let It Be" by The Beatles. As you have seen, I use a lot of rock lyrics and my writing and in my talks. I also typically have music playing while I'm working, and this day was no different. I was listening to the song, and I posted, *"When I find myself in times of trouble..."* on my page. Within a few short seconds, one of my friends responded with the comment, *"...Mother Mary comes to me."* Shortly after that someone else added, *"...speaking words of wisdom"* and then I replied with *"Let it be."* And then yet another person jumped in to start the next verse with *"In my hour of darkness."* In that moment I understood that my casual Facebook post had prompted a powerful communal connection. Prior to those moments, each of us involved in that exchange was wherever we were, doing whatever we were doing, but that post brought us all together for a time through our love of music. For me, posting lyrics is an extension of that love, so the connection I was able to make was an authentic one.

If you share what inspires you, others will be excited about it, too, and you will start an organic conversation that they will be excited to join.

Now That I Approach Facebook Strategically, I Can Share My Tips For Successful Facebook Engagement

Stop posting mundane photos or statements.

Remember, you're building a brand, which means you need to post content that will distinguish your contributions from the rest of the digital noise in people's feeds. I no longer post photos that look like everyone else's. Instead, I try to choose images that reflect where my brand journey has taken me. When I travel to exotic locations, I make a point to take crazy, colorful photos of myself in amazing surroundings. If I go on an adventure to climb a mountain or stand under a gorgeous waterfall, I take a photo to post. Live your brand, and let your social media followers see you living it!

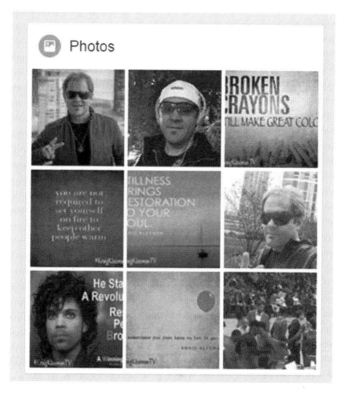

Unique images to build a winning brand.

The importance of brand cohesion applies even more directly to the images you choose as your profile picture and cover photo. They will be the first things people see when they come to your page, so give especially careful consideration to your selection of those images.

In addition to my own photos, I also have a library of hundreds of stylistic images that I put my own branding statements or taglines on, and I post them regularly on Facebook. I take care only to choose images that align with my brand messaging – images that are hopeful, for example, or that evoke a rock n' roll vibe. I have learned not to dilute my messaging by going off-brand.

An additional note: You may want to consider is turning off Facebook's photo tagging option so that you don't unwittingly end up with embarrassing photos on your Timeline if a friend tags you without thinking about how it might impact you or your business. To do this, go to the upper-right corner and click on the drop-down menu. Choose "Settings," then click on "Timeline and Tagging Settings." Set the option "Review posts friends tag you in before they appear on your timeline" to "On." Simple as that!

Facebook post with unique image and tagline.

Only post content that you and your audience will care about.

It is important to post consistently so that you stay in the minds of your audience, but you shouldn't post just for the sake of posting. Doing that will make your posts seem mundane. I focus on posting content that is positive and encouraging. I believe that words have power, and I really do think that people want to see content that is positive and hopeful. So I always post according to those beliefs. Rock lyrics definitely do resonate with a lot of people, and they are a big part of my brand, so I have continued posting those. I post lyrics that I find inspirational, and that I think others will find inspirational as well.

I also avoid posting anything polarizing or overtly political on Facebook. I don't tend to take political or religious stances in public arenas. Political discourse has its place in social media, but content that is too polarizing or negative is not what I want people to associate with my name or my brand. Similarly, I might post some content around the holidays that relates to my faith, but in general I keep my opinions on religious matters private. I'm not ashamed of my faith at all, but it is typically not explicitly related to the business topics I tend to cover. Obviously you have to find what works for you, but I would suggest that if you do post something political or religious in nature, make sure that it's relevant, both to your brand and to the cultural moment in which you're writing/posting, and that it's culturally sensitive. Again, words have power. My advice is to use positive, encouraging words and images that create a positive association with your brand.

Kraig Kleeman

Identify a "theme." This content theme should be aligned with your personal brand. In other words, think about how you want to be recognized, and make sure your content is in keeping with that theme. I have a few different themes that have been successful for me. The peace symbol is a big visual signifier of my brand, and I post a lot of photos of myself wearing my peace sign necklaces, and I post images that align with the idea of peace. I also go to a lot of Chicago Bulls games, and I post many pictures of myself at games, sometimes with my son, since we go together quite a lot. I also enjoy posting pictures from multi-generational family reunions and get-togethers because family is very important to me. I find that I get an incredible amount of "likes" when I post photos that adhere to those familiar themes. What's your theme? Are you in a creative field? Post photos of works in progress! Do you want to be seen as trustworthy and intellectual? Post links to articles on relevant topics written by well-qualified experts. Be thoughtful and deliberate about your content. Facebook even has the potential to expand your brand, as long as your posts make sense. For example, if you sell cars, and in addition to posts about cars you have to sell, you occasionally post articles about smart car technology, the place of the auto industry in the growing connectivity of the Internet of Things, or evolutions in electric cars, then you are presenting yourself as an expert on industry trends as well as a sales professional.

Don't be afraid to evolve the look and feel of your content. As we have covered, the message should continue to align with your personal brand and your skill-set. Social media are in a constant state of evolution, so you shouldn't be afraid to evolve right along with them. Since I learned to approach Facebook strategically, my influence in that channel has increased to the point where I am now having to re-think my own Facebook presence. For a while now, the number of friend requests I receive has been way beyond my ability to accept them. I hit Facebook's limit of 5,000 friends quite some time ago. At first, I went in and unfriended people that I didn't know as well to make room for new people that I knew better, but that was only a short-term solution. Now my publicist is telling me to make a public or fan page so that the friend limit won't inhibit my ability to get new followers. So, like yours, my brand journey continues to grow – my next step is to make a fan page.

Keep it simple. You don't have to write a lengthy, thought-provoking post every time you log in; in fact, it's better to keep your posts short – remember, it only took one line from a song for me to get a whole string of responses – or use photos or videos. In fact, I really advise using video. Video assets get a huge amount of traffic, and all you need is a smartphone in order to make and post one!

Ultimately, what I'm encouraging you to do is think about Facebook strategically and align your posts with the brand you are building. By now you have your own website and have begun to establish yourself as a thought leader who shares your world, and now I want you to share your world through Facebook in a strategic way.

ACTION STEPS

Having a strong presence on Facebook takes careful attention and planning. It's not enough to just make a post every once in a while because your aim is to build your Winning Brand. To do that, you need to bring the same focus and attention you used in crafting your brand initially.

Here Are Some Steps To Get You Started

Step 1: Define Your Goal

- Use SMART goal setting model (Specific, Measurable, Achievable, Realistic, Timely).
- Every post and interaction should help you accomplish your goal.
- Click a sign-up option. (NOTE: We will be using email). Enter your email information.

Step 2: Design Your Personal Brand Profile

- Select a cover image & profile image.
- Image dimensions:
  - Cover image: 851 x 351 px
  - Profile image: 180 x 180 px
- Tips: Use a stock photo for your cover image!

Step 3: Plan Carefully with a Calendar

- Use a content calendar to determine WHAT to post and WHEN.
- Tip: Look at historical data.
  - What content format has your audience responded favorably to?
  - What day of the week/time of day does your audience show the highest engagement? (Only way to find out? Trial and error!)

Step 4: Always Diversify

- No one likes to see the same thing all the time... change it up!

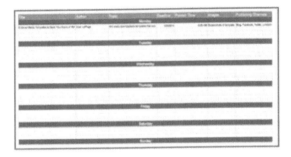

Get to know your followers. In such a vast digital landscape, people crave genuine human connection. As much as possible, give your followers individualized attention. Respond to comments, and reply to messages. If you aren't sure what types of content your followers enjoy most, feel free to engage them by asking. You can post a question for people to reply to, and Facebook even allows the use of informal polls that your followers can complete. Another way to cultivate engagement is to create and moderate a Facebook group on a topic relevant to your business or brand. This is a good way to grow your brand organically through points of common interest. You can also promote events related to your brand, or create your own, and invite your followers. You can get lots of mileage out of events because you can remind followers that the event is coming up, post from the event itself, and then post photos or reviews of the event in the days or weeks to come. The digital landscape is big, and it can be alienating, so people value connection. The more you engage your followers in a positive way, and give them a favorable brand experience, the stronger their loyalty to your brand will be.

Craft motivating, encouraging words that they will respond to.

LinkedIn Branding

I'm in with the in crowd
I go where the in crowd goes
I'm in with the in crowd And I know what
the in crowd knows Anytime of the year,
don't you hear?
Dressing fine, making time.
Dobie Gray, "The 'In' Crowd" – Billy Page

Although LinkedIn does not have as many users as Facebook, it is still one of the most important social media platforms for you to use in your brand journey. LinkedIn has more than 430 million users globally, and twenty-eight percent of adults in the Unites States log in to the site daily. You may already be quite familiar with LinkedIn, but if not, one way to describe it would be a social network for professional people. While people do post a blend of personal and professional content on both LinkedIn and Facebook, LinkedIn is more focused on business topics and professional networking.

When discussing the importance of LinkedIn, social marketing expert Jill Rowley emphasizes its power as a networking tool: "Before LinkedIn and other social networks, in the sales world, ABC stood for Always Be Closing. Now, ABC means Always Be Connecting, because your connections lead to your next hire, your next job, your next lead, and your next close." Reid Hoffman, co-founder of LinkedIn, notes that, even if you aren't actively looking for your next role, LinkedIn can help you get better at what you currently do. He says, "If you can get better at your job, you should be an active member of LinkedIn, because LinkedIn should be connecting you to the information, insights and people to be more effective." I agree with both of them wholeheartedly. You will never reach your full potential until you optimize, leverage, and harness the power of LinkedIn.

Kurt Shaver, founder of The Sales Foundry.

The next three sections of the book are adapted from videos and curriculum materials by my friend Kurt Shaver, founder of The Sales Foundry (Social Selling & LinkedIn Training for Teams), and the world's foremost expert, author, and speaker on LinkedIn. He helps people all over the world get started on LinkedIn and leverage it for their individual professional goals. His website is thesalesfoundry.com.

The next three sections contain his invaluable advice on:

1. Making a good first impression on LinkedIn.
2. Upgrading your LinkedIn brand with effective content and digital assets.
3. Building your brand credibility through recommendations.

Kraig's Experience With The Power Of LinkedIn

Aside from YouTube, LinkedIn has been the most important social medium for me in building my brand, which now extends around the whole globe in the areas of my expertise. You can do the same. In just the last three months, I have signed two major consulting engagements, one that will pay $150K, and another that will pay $200K. Both opportunities came from LinkedIn. I regularly add digital video assets to my LinkedIn profile from my YouTube channel, and in both cases the CEOs of the companies who contacted me saw my videos on LinkedIn where I talk about my approach to the sales process and sales coaching. After they read through my recommendations, researched me further, and found my website and YouTube channel, they ultimately decided to engage my services. As a direct result of my taking assets that I created for other outlets and posting them with consistency on LinkedIn, I have booked almost $350K of business this year with no sales cycle effort whatsoever.

First Impressions with LinkedIn

As much as we might like to think that we shouldn't judge a book by its cover, making a quick judgement is exactly what happens on LinkedIn. It may be unfair, but in the professional world appearances do matter. According to a survey conducted by HSN Beauty, nineteen percent of recruiters only look at the photograph when they look through profiles on LinkedIn. As Kurt Shaver says, "Everybody knows the importance of making a good first impression. As a salesperson, you might make a first impression via a face-to-face sales call, video conference call, or at a trade show or conference. Most sales professionals would not show up for one of these business meetings wearing workout sweats, a fishing vest, or with their family in tow. Don't do it with your LinkedIn photo, either." In other words, no photos with your pet. No photos with your kids. No photos of you setting a personal record at that weightlifting competition last year. Are these all important, wonderful, enriching parts of your life? Of course. Do they belong at a networking event (which, at its core, is what LinkedIn embodies in digital form)? No.

Having a recognizable and professional looking photo is key to making a good impression on LinkedIn. LinkedIn says viewers are seven times more likely to click on your profile if you have a photo. If possible, use a professional head shot. If that is not a possibility, see if you can find a friend with a good camera to take your head shot for you. Even a selfie can work in the right circumstances, if you keep some key principles in mind.

> Here are a few tips for getting an effective head shot:
>
> - Make sure your face is the focus of the photo. Remember how small profile picture are, especially on mobile devices. You are much more easily recognizable in a head shot than in a full body shot.
> - Neutral background, like a plain white wall, are the best because they put the focus on you. Avoid busy, distracting backdrops.
> - The most flattering angle is from very slightly above you. That angle emphasizes your eyes and diminishes harsh shadows.
> - Play around with lighting to find what looks best.

Whether your photo is taken by you, a friend, or a professional, it is important to make sure that it looks like you. Remember, building a brand means building credibility. New connections will look you up before interviews, meetings or important events, and the person who shows up should be the same person they are expecting. This is why it's important, not only that the photo emphasize your face, but that the photo be up to date. If you have changed your hair color, gotten glasses, stopped wearing glasses, altered the way you wear your facial hair, or gained or lost a significant amount of weight, it's probably time for a new photo.

To post a profile picture on your LinkedIn account, go to the "Profile" tab at the top of the page. Making the selection there will give you the opportunity to select "Edit Profile" from the drop-down menu. You will notice the yellow cropping box that you can use in case your photo is larger than the allotted head shot size on LinkedIn. And on the right side of the screen, you will see that it shows you the preview of what the photo will look like once it is cropped. If you need to change the photo size (the minimum size for photos on LinkedIn is now 200x200 pixels), you can click on "Change photo." You'll know that you're in edit mode because you'll see the small pencil icons next to the text fields and the camera icon next to the photo. If you click on the camera icon, you'll see that it gives you the chance to choose another photo. When you have selected and sized your photo, just click "Save." It's good to do this in the middle of the business day because your connections will get notified you have a new photo, and that's a good chance to raise your visibility.

In addition to a good headshot, it is important to use the headline field in an effective way. The headline is limited to 120 characters, so it forces you to be succinct. In order to conceptualize your headline, it can be helpful to first open a document in a word processing program while you compose your statement. If you have room for your title and company name, it's a good idea to include those, especially if you work for a company that has a well-recognized and respected brand. But I suggest starting by writing out a customer-oriented benefits statement. Your headline will be a variation on *"I help* _____ *to do* _____*,"* in which you fill in the first blank with the type of customers or audience you work with, and then fill in the second blank with how you benefit them. For example, a headline for an insurance professional could be: *"Account executive with XYZ Corp. I help mid-sized construction companies protect their business."* We still have some room left, so we could add a bit more depth and try, *"Account executive with XYZ Corp. I help mid-sized construction companies protect their business and manage employee benefits."* This, unfortunately, puts us over the character limit, so we would need to edit a bit. Since "benefits" in an insurance context implies "employee benefits," we can remove "employee," and we are left with "Account executive with XYZ Corp. I help mid-sized construction companies protect their business and manage benefits." Now that we have our headline, we copy the text. Then we go to "Edit profile" and go to the icon of the edit pencil next to the "Your professional headline" field and paste in our new headline.

Making A Great First Impression – Key Takeaways

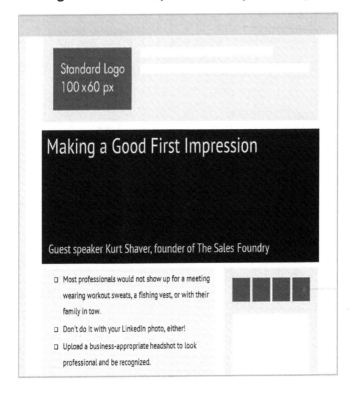

Upgrading Your LinkedIn Brand

LinkedIn has added the capacity for users to add media assets to dress up their profiles. Video is a vitally important asset in boosting your brand visibility and credibility, especially if you post videos of you shining at what you do best – perhaps giving a talk at a conference, or presenting at a client engagement, or delivering some clever industry insights into your camera phone or GoPro. According to <u>Forbes</u>, sixty-five percent of executives have visited a vendor's website after watching a video, and 39% of those executives have called a vendor after watching a video. According to Dr. James McQuivey of Forrester Research, *"a minute of video is worth 1.8 million words."* In order to fully leverage the power of LinkedIn, I strongly encourage you to embrace the impact that video has in the digital landscape.

In order to post a video, go to the tool bar at the top of the page, and click on "Edit profile." One place you can add media is in the summary section. Click on the square icon, and you will see that the site gives you two ways to add media assets. You can add a link or upload a file up to 100 megabytes, which is good for images or for a PowerPoint slide, perhaps from a presentation you have given. The site allows you to give it a title and brief summary. The other option is to add video, which is perhaps the most impactful type of media asset you can use. LinkedIn does not host videos for its users, but you can paste in the link to your video from YouTube, Vimeo, or whatever site hosts your video. All the viewer needs to do to view the video is click on the link.

As with Facebook, you will need to experiment to see what frequency and times of posting elicit the best response from your connections.

Communicate Your Personal Brand – Key Takeaways

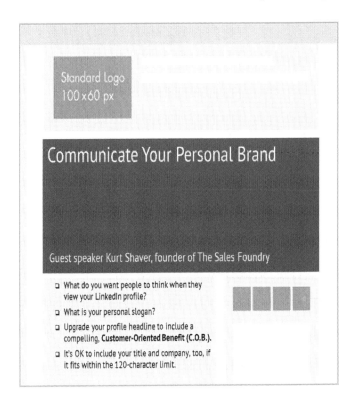

Building Your Brand Credibility

Once you set up or revise your profile, start expanding your digital network by inviting people you know to connect with you. When LinkedIn offers to show you *"people you may know,"* click through and see who you can invite to connect from that list. Don't just send invitations to connect to everyone you find on LinkedIn, though. People looking at your profile will judge you in part by who is in your network, so make sure you're your professional connections are ones that make sense for your brand. Another good way to make connections in an organic way is to join groups related to causes you believe in or to your professional interest areas. Post comments or ask thoughtful questions in those groups to invite conversation and get more engagement with associates or clients you'd like to work with.

As on Facebook, you have the option to "like" or share links or articles on LinkedIn, and doing so helps you to stay visible on your connections' feeds. Share articles relevant to your field, and comment on the content shared by others.

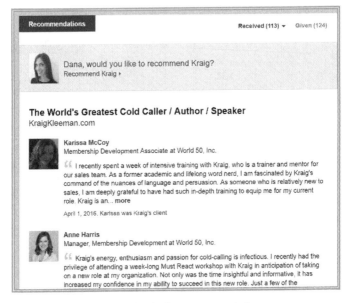

Example of LinkedIn recommendation.

Another important way to leverage LinkedIn is by requesting recommendations from your level one connections. (LinkedIn categorizes connections by degrees: 1st, 2nd, and 3rd, with first being someone you are directly connected to, and second being someone connected to one of your connections, and so on. LinkedIn only allows you to request recommendations from your level one connections). Much like in the non-digitized world, recommendations carry a lot of weight. In fact, the most important metric for your LinkedIn profile is how many recommendations you have and from how many different companies. When you're looking to brand yourself, you want to have as many recommendations from as many different industries as possible. This method shows that you have broad appeal, and avoids any appearance that you may have used undue influence to pressure coworkers or direct reports at one company to recommend you.

Here's how you request a recommendation from a level 1 connection. If you are in sales, it is best to ask a former customer that you have provided extraordinary service to. Click on "Edit profile," and scroll down to the recommendations section, which is pretty far down on the profile. Click on the small blue pencil icon, and then on "Ask to be recommended." Then the site will take you step by step through: 1) What role you want to be recommended for (choose from the drop-down menu), and 2) Who do you want to ask to recommend you, what your relationship was, and what their role was at the time you worked or did business together. LinkedIn then tees up a message requesting a recommendation. I suggest that you take the time to personalize the message to remind the potential recommender about your experience doing business together, and make it easier for them to write something meaningful. Once you finish your message, click send. Then all you have to do is wait for them to write the referral, and, once they send it, you just accept it to post to your profile.

LinkedIn is, without a doubt, the most important business-oriented social media platform, and it is one that I want you to participate in with strength. It is more than just a digital place to post your resume; it is also a place for personal branding. Every connection, every endorsement, every comment you make in a group discussion, every video or link you post will become part of your brand. For my own LinkedIn presence, I do post some entertainment content because I want people to see that side of me, and because music-related links are consistent with my brand. Don't think of LinkedIn as a just a stuffy business channel. As we have discussed, you want to curate your content carefully so that it doesn't detract or distract from the credibility of your brand. But don't be afraid to make an occasional bold post. In the examples from my own business that I just mentioned, those executives noticed my content, and they came to me. As I like to say, sometimes you have to bust a move so you can improve!

ACTION STEPS

LinkedIn is a very powerful tool in building your brand, so carefully build your LinkedIn presence and build your network by regularly expanding your reach, thereby building your influence.

Brand-building exercise:

- Do online research and find one news story that you can post on LinkedIn that would be relevant to your brand. In one sentence explain why you chose that link.
- Now, find one serious video – perhaps an instructional video or a Ted Talk - that you can post that would be relevant to your brand. In

one sentence explain why you chose that video.

- Bonus Bust-a-Move assignment: Find one fun entertainment link – a clip from a concert, a music video, a funny animal video – that you could post.

- If you are new to LinkedIn, name five people you plan to connect with once you create your account. Make a task for yourself to invite those five people to connect the same day you have your profile ready for viewing.

- Name one person you plan to ask for a recommendation.

Building Brand Credibility – Key Takeaways

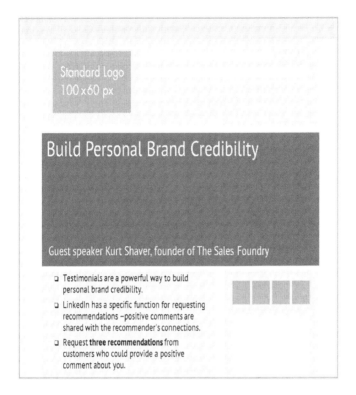

Show Your Digital Assets

It's your tomorrow
Right now,
C'mon, it's everything
Right now,
Catch a magic moment,
do it Right here and now.
"Right Now," Van Halen – For Unlawful Carnal Knowledge

As you begin to establish your presence on the various social media channels that you have now registered for, you will need a library of assets to post so that you can stay consistently engaged with the audience you are building. Just having the accounts doesn't do you any good; you have to **use** them! Here are four steps to making your content part of your winning brand strategy:

Step 1. Get to know your audience

Get to know them by engaging with them, and by experimenting with posts on different days, at different times, that feature different types of content. Only through trial and error can you discover what your audience responds to the best.

Step 2. Try different types of content

If there is one type you find you are really good at, do not be afraid to focus your efforts in one area. According to Content Marketing Institute, the most effective content marketers use an average of 15 different approaches! See what your audience likes best. Some common approaches, broken down by purpose, include:

To Entertain & Build Awareness: Competition and Quizzes

According to Noah Kagan of Huffington Post, Facebook reposting showed that "eight of the top 10 most shared articles in the past eight months were quizzes (seven from BuzzFeed, one from the *NY Times*). Why quizzes? Because when we share our quiz results, it fuels our identity and ego. Others will learn more about who we are, what we value, and our tastes." You can entertain and get to know your audience better at the same time.

To Entertain & Build an Emotional Connection: Viral Content and Videos or Images

According to the same Huffington Post study, twice as many Facebook users will re-post content if it contains at least one image. Images, videos, and song lyrics resonate with people on an emotional level, which will in turn create a stronger sense of connection to your brand.

To Inspire & Drive Purchase: Celebrity Endorsements and Client Reviews

The psychology behind this premise is called social proof. The idea is that people will do what others do because they assume that what others are doing must be right or appropriate. For example, if you get to a venue and see everyone standing in a line, chances are you'll get in the line because you assume that the line is how you get inside. Sharing positive reviews from clients or business associates is a good way to use social proof to your advantage and boost the credibility of your brand. Statistics say that 85-90% of online buyers are influenced by reviews in making their purchasing decisions. Think about it – have you bought anything on Amazon without at least glancing at the reviews? And, of course, celebrity endorsements don't hurt either. Being able to associate your brand with people who are perceived as influencers is a big bonus. When Ellen Degeneres pulled out her Samsung and took that famous Oscar selfie backstage in 2014 with Brad Pitt, Bradley Cooper, Meryl Streep, Jennifer Lawrence and other A-list stars, that photo was retweeted three million times. According to *Search Engine Journal*, it was estimated to be worth between $800 million and $1 billion to Samsung. Another example is how Mark Zuckerberg casually mentioned his iGrill in a Facebook post and inadvertently drove so much traffic to the company's web site that it crashed. I have mentioned before how I have been fortunate enough to have Bono's endorsement as the foreword to my book. My Bono story paved the way to increased success for me, which opened up further opportunities, such as meeting Tony Blair, which continues to yield still more opportunities.

To Educate & Demonstrate Rational: Press Releases and Guides

If you want your followers to know about a contest you're running, a workshop you're moderating, or a talk you're giving, you can post a press release to publicize your event. Another form of informative content is a guide. For example, I've written blog entries, which you can access through my website kraigkleeman.com, with such titles as "3 Tips for Exceptional Customer Service" and "Top 4 Email Fails" in order to educate my followers on the topics they seek me out for.

To Convince & Demonstrate Rationale: Demo Videos and Case Studies

Another form of content is to post demo videos and case studies. Videos tend to get people's attention, and it is often helpful for people to see how something is done rather than just read about it. Also, viewers get to know you a bit better; they get to hear your voice, see how you work, perhaps see parts of the space you work in, all of which makes them feel more connected to you. Case studies can also be effective because they make abstract knowledge concrete. They enable you to show how you were able to help a particular client, a client who faced challenges that your followers may be able to relate to.

Step 3. Stay true to yourself

As we have discussed, if you post content that genuinely represents you, then your audience will look forward to seeing it. If you post something out of character, your followers will find it jarring and perhaps even upsetting. Remember, as you build your brand, make sure that it's something you can live up to so that you will find it easy to stay consistent.

Step 4. Establish a pattern/frequency

Based on the content you are using, how often are you going to post on each platform? Once you establish what pattern works best, make a commitment to stick to it. Keep your audience's attention and goodwill by following through on the content they come to expect from you. We citizens of this digital world have increasingly short attention spans, so you don't want your followers to have a chance to forget about you.

Step 5. Make a content calendar

Schedule and plan your posts in advance. Before I began my brand journey, I just posted whatever I felt like posting in the moment, but posting with intention and mindfulness isn't that simple. Writing takes time. So does finding the right moment to capture in a photo, or making a short video where you deliver industry insights to your audience, or tracking down a relevant quotation to repost. Also, if you plan out your content in advance, it makes it easier to plan a variety of types of content because you won't be grasping for something at the last minute. You can also make provisions ahead of time for those occasions when you'll be away from your computer. It is incredibly helpful to have a rich inventory of content to draw on.

People who are involved in my online course *A Winning Brand* have access to dozens of templates that you can customize and distribute throughout all of your social media channels. If you find you need more than what we have provided, you can order additional templates – we have hundreds in our digital library. They are ready for you to customize them with your own tagline for your own branding posts, just like I put "The World's Greatest Cold Caller" or "Kraig-KleemanTV" or "The Business of Life" on the ones I post.

Example of a branded image template.

All of the templates we provide lend themselves well to expressions of inspiration. As I've mentioned, I believe in putting positive vibes out into the world.

Positive images and messages tend to generate positive responses.

The templates are in PowerPoint, so once you get PowerPoint up and running, you will select a template from the available files included with your course material. In order to add your personalized text, you first highlight the default or existing text on the template, so that you maintain the integrity of the formatting. Then you click in the area and type in your own text. You can make adjustments to suit your preferences. For example, you can adjust the positioning or the color of the text. Be sure to select text that your audience will feel is important. If you use an inspirational quotation, make sure it's one that supports your brand narrative.

Next, you will update your logo or brand tagline. Click on the "Format" tab on the toolbar across the top, and then click on "Change Picture." You will then go into your files and exchange the existing image for your own image or logo. Then you click into the box for the tagline at the lower left, and type in your personal tagline. To save the entire image, we highlight every aspect of our image. Click your mouse and select around your entire image. If for some reason your whole background was not selected, hold down your shift key and click the background, and you should see the background highlighted. The next thing to do is back-click so that your options open in a drop-down menu. Select "save as picture." Then save your file in a safe place, such as your desk top or on a thumb drive, or wherever your other images are.

Pablo by Buffer editing platform.

A great free online tool that anyone can use is Pablo by Buffer, which is a big help in crafting the engaging social media content necessary to boost your personal brand engagement. No design experience is necessary.

In fact, you don't even need to sign in to the site. Just go to www.pablo.buffer.com, and click the blue button that says "Try Pablo *it's free!*" Next, you will be able to search through all of their materials and select the template, quote, announcement, promotion, outreach, etc. that is most appropriate for you and your personal brand. Then you can choose an image for the asset you have chosen. There are fifty thousand stock images on the site that are free to use. Once you choose your image, select the size for social media uploading – the logos at the top right will guide you to the correct size for each particular platform, whether it is Pinterest, Instagram, Facebook, or Twitter. Then you can choose a filter. Afterward, fill in your text in the appropriate field. You can make your text a header, body, or caption placement, and you can change the typeface, the size or the color. Then you just need to download your work. Another useful feature is that Pablo comes preloaded with a treasure trove of quotations, so if you're having writer's block but would like to post something quickly, you just add a preloaded quote and post it to your social media channels. Just that easily, you will have kept up with your desired posting schedule.

As you can see, reaching your audience with quality content on a consistent basis takes time and effort, but cultivating a strong content library will empower you to reach your audience with the right messaging at the right time.

ACTION STEPS

Building a library of brand assets to use for your social media profiles will ensure a fresh, consistent flow of content for your followers. Attention spans are short and expectations are high, so taking the time to build a quality library with a variety of assets will keep your followers coming back and looking to you as an expert.

Gather or develop a library of different posts, including posts:

- To entertain & build awareness: competitions and quizzes

119

- To entertain & build an emotional connection: viral content and videos or images
- To inspire & drive purchase: celebrity endorsements and client reviews
- To educate & demonstrate rational: press releases and guides
- To convince & demonstrate rational: demo videos and case studies

Next, develop a content calendar that will allow you schedule posts ahead of time.

Quick 5-Step Recap

Step 1

Select a background (template) within this document.

Step 2

Add interesting text - make sure to use unique content audience will care about.

Step 3

Update with your personal brand image or logo.

Step 4

Update with your personal brand tagline.

Step 5

Save the individual slide as an image and post social media!

Twitter Tips
And Strategies

Twitter is another popular social media platform where you can build a winning brand to help you create enormous influence and potentially earn millions. It has over 300 million users worldwide. Unlike Facebook or LinkedIn, where you use your real-world connections to start building your online social network, Twitter enables you to connect with anyone in the world who has a Twitter account.

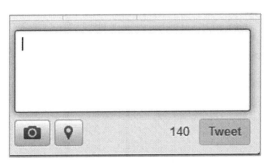

Think outside of the 140 character limit.

As Pete Cashmore, founder of the Mashable website, says, *"We're living at a time when attention is the new currency,"* and Twitter has the capacity to get you attention from people you would never reach otherwise, from people who live in distant countries to celebrities and powerful executives. Twitter also differs from the other two platforms in that users post more frequently, and so they tend to get responses to their content more quickly. Twitter is a constant flow of countless global conversations, and once you join the platform, you can participate in the conversations that interest you. Another unique feature of Twitter, one that may make it seem intimidating or limiting at first, is that it restricts the length of any individual post – or, as posts are called on Twitter, any individual "tweet" – to 140 characters.

I don't mind admitting that I had mixed feelings about Twitter at first because of that character limit. I tend to be kind of a nerd about topics that matter to me, and I like to develop my thoughts fully and deeply, in a professional and sometimes even academic way. I enjoy making fully developed, persuasive arguments backed by solid evidence. That level of discourse is impossible in such a short format. Once I saw how popular Twitter was becoming, though, I realized how important that medium would be for reaching and relating to my audience. I decided that it would be a fun exercise to challenge myself to be that brief. So even though I struggled at first, I began to think of content I could post that went beyond argumentative thought and instead focused on topics that are trending, which is to say, topics that are the most popular among users at a given moment. Trending topics are often driven by world events, such as the death of a famous person, a celebrity wedding, a political election, a major sporting event, or the opening week of a summer blockbuster. Have you heard that quote about how a man never steps in the same river twice, because both the man and the river are always changing? That's true of Twitter as well. The conversational flow of tweets is constantly growing and evolving and offering new opportunities to engage. That's a huge benefit to you as you begin to engage; you will never run out of conversations you can join, or comments you can make. It can be a bit easier to say something succinct about a topic of the day than about something deeply philosophical. I created a strategy of content within 140 characters, and I began using the images that I developed – the same kind that we are teaching you to build for yourself. I also began to tweet at people at other companies or blogs whom I had done business with or had met at conferences I attended. And as I did that, they would retweet or favorite my tweets. To recap, I suggest following three principles:

1. Don't feel constricted by the character limit – instead, let it inspire your creativity
2. Use impactful images to increase follower engagement
3. Tweet at influencers to engage them and build rapport

Once I started sticking to these principles, my following on Twitter accelerated exponentially; I went from zero followers to over twenty-nine thousand! In this chapter I will guide you through getting started on Twitter, as well as some tips and recommended practices.

Steps For Establishing A Successful Twitter Presence

Step 1.

As with other social media platforms, use the S.M.A.R.T. goal-setting model. Set goals that are:
- Specific
- Measurable
- Achievable
- Realistic, and
- Timely

Step 2.

Design your Twitter personal brand profile.
1. Select a header image that aligns with your brand message.
   - Not Sure what picture to pick for your cover image? Use a stock photo.
   - You can find great stock photos on this site: pixabay.com.
2. Select a profile photo as well.
3. Edit your bio.

Make sure any files you upload do not exceed 3 MB. Re-structure your profile design for Twitter's new design dimensions:

Header Photo: 1500 pixels by 500 pixels
  - File size (maximum) of 10 MB
  - File type should be JPG, GIF or PNG

Profile Photo: 500 pixels by 500 pixels
  - 400 x 400 pixels (minimum)
  - Square iamge is recommended
  - File size (maximum) of 100 KB
  - File type should be JPG, GIF or PNG

Tweeted Image: 1024 pixels by 1024 pixels
  - 440 x 220 pixels (minimum)
  - When photo is selected and expanded,
       Minimum : *440 pixels by 220 pixels*
       Maximum : *1024 pixels by 512 pixels*
  - File size (maximum) of 5 MB for photos
  - File size (maximum) of 3 MB for animated GIFs

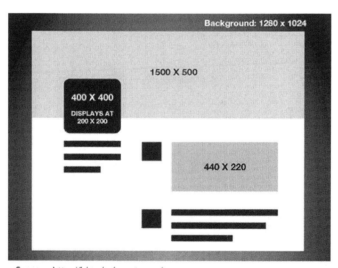

Source: http://blog.hubspot.com/

Step 3.

Use a social media calendar. Find out what works and doesn't work; post accordingly!

Step 4.

Increase engagement with the following strategies:

- **Say "Thank you!"** Thank someone who shares your content or retweets you! treating people with respect is always a good practice in both the digital and non-digital world, and it helps you build a good reputation. That person may be more likely to retweet you again. Also, expressing gratitude may open up an avenue further interaction.
- **Retweet Your Followers** Twitter is a conversation, not an echo chamber; interaction is the name of the game. Choose tweets that align with your brand's values and add a comment to contribute.
- **Ask Questions** Have a conversation with your followers by posting questions and responding. In such a huge digital arena, personal connection makes a big impact and can establish the foundation for brand loyalty.
- **Know Your Followers** Get to know your followers. Craft motivating, encouraging words they would respond to.
- **Cross Promote Your Content** Embed your twitter feed into your website to make it easy for your audience to see.

Step 5.

Keep followers interested by:

- Pulling your content from all different sources.
- Making sure you are not entirely self-promoting.
- Letting your personality SHINE! Use a combination of funny, serious content and images.
- Mixing it up a little bit – make sure to interact with your followers as well!
- Solving a problem to help your followers

While Following The Five Steps, Keep These Twitter Tips In Mind

Twitter Tips

1. Think beyond 140 characters & think about that are trending.
2. Add images, GIFs, & videos.
3. Use Hashtags # that are relevant to you personally.

Twitter Strategies

1. Create a strategy of content using 140 characters.
2. Use creative images.
3. Tweet @ important people in your network. As you begin to tweet @ influencers, these individuals of high importance will re-tweet your posts.
4. Most importantly, let go of your preconceived ideas about communicating on Twitter and enjoy the experience.

I hope you are able to benefit from the lesson I learned on my own journey with Twitter. First, don't be intimidated or annoyed by the character limit. Instead, let the constraints inspire you to get creative. In fact, you may want to train yourself to be even briefer than that - according to statistics cited by Belle Beth Cooper in her article "10 Surprising New Twitter Stats to Help You Reach More Followers" on *Huffington Post*, tweets with fewer than one hundred characters get seventeen percent more engagement. I also encourage you to add images, GIFs (short animations), or videos to your tweets. Cooper's article also reveals that tweets with images get twice as much engagement as those without, which is good for relating to followers you already have, and tweets with links are eighty-six percent more likely to be retweeted, which can be useful to know when you are trying to establish or broaden your reach. As you build your following on Twitter, you will want to keep those two separate metrics in mind: engagement from existing followers, and your follower count. The tactics to increase one may not necessarily increase the other, so, as I have mentioned, experimentation and tracking are important.

Finally, I recommend that you get in the habit of using hashtags to highlight key words that are relevant to you and your brand. If you are new to Twitter, you may not yet know that you can create a short link by putting a pound sign (#) in front of a word or phrase. For example, if you're watching the American Music Awards, you might tweet about something you see and use the hashtag #AMAs. Hashtags I might use with a tweet about a sales training engagement might include #salestraining or #sales. When you use a hashtag, your tweet feeds into that grouping of tweets and becomes searchable by that term. The hashtag is what lets you join the conversation about that particular topic. Hashtags are a great way to connect with people who are interested in or commenting on the same topics as you. It important to use them wisely, though. Make sure the hashtags you implement are relevant to you and your brand. If you use a popular hashtag that is unrelated to your brand just to get people's attention, you risk losing credibility. Also, stay focused and avoid using too many hashtags; statistic show that, while tweets with hashtags get twice as much engagement as those without, limiting yourself to one or two gets you twenty-one percent more engagement than using three or more.

I will leave you with a final list of four strategies that I recommend you use to make your brand a powerful presence in what has come to be called the Twitter-verse:

1. Create a strategy of content using 140 characters.

2. Use creative images.

3. Tweet at important people in your network. When you use the @ symbol in front of a user's Twitter handle, you are addressing that person or company directly. For example, my handle is @Kraig_Kleeman. Most people use some variation of their name, but some are playful. Jason Grilli, pitcher for the Pittsburgh Pirates, uses the handle @GrillCheese49. As I mentioned earlier, one of the great things about Twitter is that you can reach or address anyone who is a fellow user. As CEO and co-founder of Twitter Jack Dorsey says, "What's interesting about Twitter and the influencers that someone follows – like, say, Shaquille O'Neal – is that they see someone who is us-

ing the exact same tools that they have access to, and I think that inspires this hope to be able to really engage with someone like him."

As you begin to tweet @ influencers, these individuals of high importance will re-tweet your posts, which is not only a thrill but will also build your credibility and expand your influence.

4. Most importantly, let go of your preconceived ideas about communicating on Twitter, and enjoy the experience!

ACTION STEPS

To optimize your Twitter presence, complete the following exercise.

Brand-building exercise:

- Do some research and name five hashtags that you think would be useful to your brand. They can relate to your area of business, a cultural event that relates to your industry, a cause you support, etc.

- For each hashtag, write a sample tweet – remember to keep it at 140 characters or less – that you can imagine yourself posting.

- Name five influencers – major figures in your field, actors, athletes, musicians – that you could tweet "@" on Twitter, whose image would enhance your brand if you could associate it with them.

Kraig Kleeman

Organizing Your Social Media Outreach With Hootsuite

Manage all of your accounts in one place.

Before we go any further, I want to acknowledge that it can be a bit daunting for a beginner to think about managing all of these social media accounts. If you're feeling intimidated or over-whelmed, don't worry! There are great tools out there called Social Media

135

Management Software (SMMS) to help you stay orga-
nized while creating personal connections through
social media. The tool I personally prefer to use is
called Hootsuite. It is free to use, and it is a great solution to help you manage your social media activity.
There are paid upgrades available, but most users find
that the free version meets their needs. You can build
lots of content in advance, and you can schedule it to
go out on a regular basis.

To sign up for Hootsuite, go to **www.hootsuite.com
/plans**, and continue by selecting the green button
labeled "Get Started – Free." Complete the fields, and
click "Create Account." To continue with Hootsuite,
your social media accounts must all be authorized.
Click on each one, and choose who you want your
posts to be shared with (the "public" setting will obviously have the broadest reach). Select "Ok" and
continue. On the right side of the screen, you will see
a tracker that shows how much time you have saved
by using Hootsuite. Just by authorizing Facebook,
Hootsuite indicates that you will save twenty minutes
a day, 2.3 hours a week, and five days a year. Repeat

this authorization process for each social network, and, when you are done adding them, select the big green button that says "Done adding social networks." Once you are in the system, you can start using it right away to post content.

Hootsuite integrates with all of the social media platforms I cover here, as well as some lesser used ones. It connects to Facebook, Twitter, LinkedIn, Google+, Instagram, YouTube, Foursquare, WordPress, MySpace, and Mixi. Hootsuite is a useful tool that you can leverage to engage with your audience in a way that will make it easier to boost your brand.

ACTION STEPS

Set up your Hootsuite account to make it easier to regularly communicate with your social media followers be completing the following steps:

Visit www.hootsuite.com/plans

Select the green button: "Get Started-Free"

Type your information in the fields and click: "Create Account"

Connect Hootsuite to social networks of your choice by providing authorization

Get started with Hootsuite – plan, post, and track!

Instagram And Brand Engagement

"Every picture tells a story, don't it?"
– "Every Picture Tells a Story" Rod Stewart,
Every Picture Tells a Story (1971)

Instagram is another popular social media platform that is free to use, and it is important to have a branded presence there. If you are not yet familiar with Instagram, it is a mobile application that allows users to shoot, edit and share photos or videos straight from their phones. Like Twitter, on Instagram you can follow celebrities, brands, and friends to view their photos. Instagram enjoys even more popularity than Twitter, with over 400 million users worldwide.

Monthly users are up 35% month over month and growing! According to Search Engine Watch, 27.6% of Americans use Instagram, and 35% of users accessed Instagram several times a day as of April 2015.

It is probably most convenient to use Instagram on your mobile device. You can download the app by getting it from Apple's App Store or from Google Play.

It is simple to use Instagram in a meaningful way if you follow these important steps. You have the option to do sign up with your email or Facebook account. Because Facebook now owns Instagram, one benefit of signing up through your Facebook account is that your existing Facebook contacts will populate in your Instagram, and any images that you post can be shared easily across both platforms. If you are new to Instagram, just fill out all the required fields and click "Sign up." When you create your account, you will fill out information related to your brand, including your profile picture, user name, and bio.

Step 1. Sign up!

Be sure to make your username RECOGNIZABLE so that you are easily searchable.
- Set your profile to PUBLIC by clicking "Options".
- Make sure the "Private Account" toggle is off.

Step 2. Set up your account

Define your goal - how will you be using Instagram to reach your audience?
- Will it be used to... increase your personal brand awareness?
- Will it be used to... show your audience what you are great at?
- Will it be used to... share your interests and/or passions with your audience?

Each piece you post should add value to your personal brand and help accomplish the goal.
- Select an on-brand profile image.
- Add your bio... remember to stay true to your personal brand's personality. Create a short bio that captures your brand story or vision and, ideally, also includes a link to your website.
- Here are a few examples of bold brand bios: somup.com/cDeeFCtV7

The following are excellent examples of Instagram brand bios.

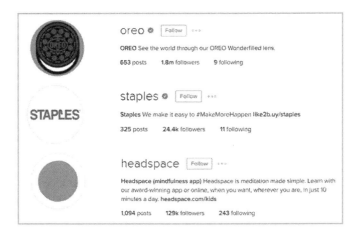

These are all good examples of brand bios because they exemplify each company's vision and mission, and I challenge you to do the same.

Create compelling and engaging content that your followers will enjoy, and that will accomplish your goal. Instagram content contains two main parts: beautiful images and compelling text.

Beautiful Images:
- 1080 x 566 pixels (minimum)
- 1080 x 1350 pixels (maximum)

Compelling Text:
- A question which can boost the number of comments from viewers
- A compelling quotation
- A call to action, such as asking viewers to "like" the post or tag someone

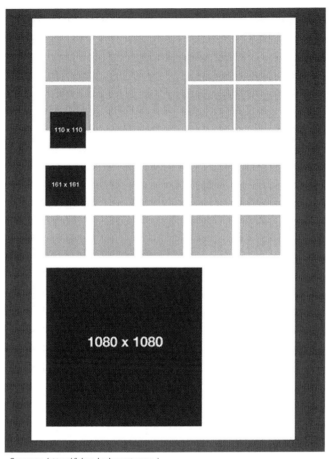

Source: http://blog.hubspot.com/

Step 3. Snap your shots

Here is a list of databases containing these royalty-free images:
- Negative Space (negativespace.co)
- Death to the Stock Photo (deathtothestockphoto.com)
- Picjumbo (picjumbo.com)
- Kaboompics (kaboompics.com)

Start with an awesome photo. We have seen that in other social media platforms, posts that contain an image tend to get more engagement. Instagram is obviously the most image-centric of the social media platforms, so you will want to take extra care not to settle for images that are mundane or unremarkable. Instagram is popular because people love pictures. Also, remember that most people will be scrolling through Instagram on their phones. To get an inspiring photo, you can take it yourself or use a stock photo. Instagram has a lot of fun filters and features that allow you to create interesting effects on the photos you take. Sometimes you can make an everyday object seem fresh just by playing around with filters. Fortunately, there are countless royalty-free stock photos you can use without worrying about violating copyright laws. Whether you take a photo yourself or select one from a database, make sure that the image is consistent with your brand. If you run a yoga studio, for example, you can post photos of how you set up your space for a workshop or import an image of a lotus or a still pond. If you are in sales, you might post images of your product or people using your product. People also like to see behind-the-scenes action, so think about snapping photos of the set-up for an event, or of your staff when you take them out to a special dinner.

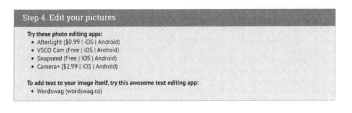

If you follow those steps, you will be on your way to establishing a successful brand presence on Instagram. It may also be useful to know that some of the conventions of Twitter and Facebook apply to Instagram. You can tag individual users in your posts, for example. Also, as on Twitter, you can – and should – implement hashtags in order to reach more users. But, again as on Twitter, don't get carried away! Avoid using long lists of hashtags, as they risk obscuring the main message of your content and your brand. You can find people to follow, just as you would on Twitter, by searching hashtags related to your interests. If you don't know where to start, you can even use the "Suggested Users" feature, which appears on a drop-down menu under "Find & Invite Friends."

And don't forget the power of video assets! Instagram now allows you to upload videos of up to sixty seconds. In addition, in early 2016 Instagram added a feature that allows you to click on the view count for a video and see how many times it has been viewed for at least 3 seconds, so that you can track your followers' engagement with those assets.

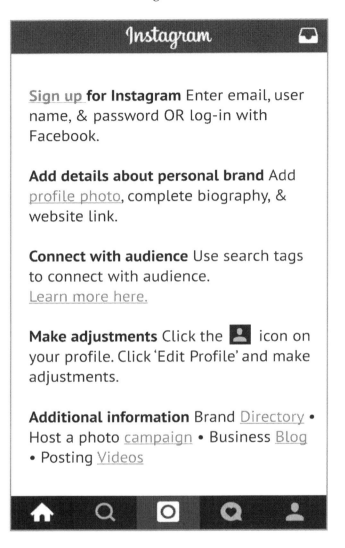

Finally, I encourage you to go the extra mile in reaching and relating to your followers! One way to get people involved is to run an Instagram contest.

You can run a contest to:

- Boost reach
- Encourage retweets
- Attract new followers
- Increase @mentions of your brand's Instagram and/or Twitter handle

One idea for a contest is to ask followers to submit a photo or answer a question. Asking your followers to submit a photo deepens the connection they have to your brand because it prompts them to actively engage and co-create rather than passively consume content. Another option is to encourage followers to use a specific hashtag (#) to enter your contest. Create an incentive that, if they use that hashtag, they are eligible to win a prize voucher. As you should do with every step in your branding journey, though, be deliberate about what you want to accomplish. Are you hoping to get a certain number of uses for a particular hashtag? Increase your number of followers by a certain amount? What segment of Instagram users are you trying to reach with your brand, and how does your contest strategy engage them? What kind of prize can you offer that is meaningful to them and also relevant to your brand vision? Then, once the contest ends, be sure to thank the participants. This is another opportunity to engage them, and you also want to make your followers feel appreciated when they make an effort to connect with you. Then share the award-winning entry so that the winning follower feels extra special, and so that you can keep the momentum that you've built going after the contest ends.

ACTION STEPS

Once you've registered for n Instagram account, it's time to build your followers, and the following steps will help make that easier.

Brand-building exercise:

- Choose three images from one of the stock-photo resources mentioned in this book that you could use for your Instagram feed. In one sentence state why those images represent your brand. What emotions do they evoke? What text would you pair each image with and why? How does the image reinforce the text you plan to use?

- Using your personal brand tagline form earlier in the book as a starting point, come up with two possible brand bios to use on Instagram. Show them to trusted friends or colleagues and ask for feedback. Which one is stronger and why?

Building
YouTube Success

YouTube is one of the most powerful platforms you can use in building a winning brand. It is a great way for you to share your expertise with the world. According to Forbes.com, there are over 1 billion unique visits to YouTube every month. According to YouTube's own statistics, the number of people watching each day has grown forty percent year-over-year since March 2016. Those numbers represent tremendous opportunity!

KraigKleemanTV episode on YouTube.

When I first started using YouTube, I was frightened and reserved, both about appearing on video and about committing to the creation of a large body of video content. But I can tell you without reservation that beginning to create videos was a pivotal moment in building my brand. I hadn't thought of using video until my brand started growing through the other social media channels I was using, and a friend came to me and said, "Your brand is becoming so strong, that if you create a channel and start pumping out the content you have already created on your topics of expertise, your brand will soar." I told him I would do it if he would help me get started, and he did. I started with just my iPhone and a small tripod, and I filmed my first videos on my balcony. Just as you already have expertise in your subject areas, I already had content that I had produced in my areas of expertise. I just needed to translate it into video format. So I mounted my phone, made sure the lighting was good, and started making instructional videos around the topic of sales processes, sales transformation, and also sales techniques for managers and executives. As easily as that, my YouTube channel – KraigKleemanTV –

was born. The style of my videos has definitely matured over time; for example, later on, I started adding music, a branded backdrop, and then an intro and outro. But those more sophisticated touches came later. At first it was just me and my iPhone. I have to tell you that the best investment in my YouTube journey was buying a GoPro. I now take it with me everywhere I go to make my videos.

Video has been a game changer for me, and it can be for you, too.

First, find your content. What is your area of expertise? What subjects do people seek your advice on? Speak on those topics.

Second, find a style that is part of your brand, so that your video content will be consistent with the rest of your social media efforts.

Do you need high-energy video with bright colors or fast music? What kinds of backgrounds do you want to use? What kinds do you have access to? A classic, minimalist background? Does being outdoors fit your brand? Presenting in front of a whiteboard? What do you plan to wear? Is your speech style upbeat or more deliberate? Think carefully about how the format, visual elements, and sound all contribute to your messaging.

Finally, just get started! In my view, YouTube is the place to put your content because of its huge user base, but Vimeo offers a great option for professional videos as well. If you take the time to create a channel and to film yourself, you can exponentially increase your influence. Whereas once I was afraid of filming myself for YouTube, I am now negotiating for a full-blown studio. So don't be afraid – be bold, and let go of your inhibitions! As I've mentioned before, just as Rod Stewart says that every picture tells a story, I say that every video tells a thousand stories.

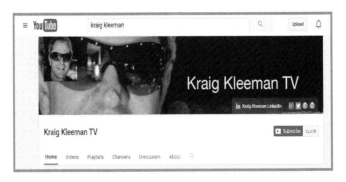

Professional branding on Kraig Kleeman TV YouTube Channel.

In fact, video is powerful enough that some people have risen to fame and fortune exclusively through that format. Love him or hate him, Justin Bieber was discovered on YouTube. Michelle Phan, founder of the $500 million beauty subscription business Ipsy, got her start doing makeup tutorials on YouTube in 2007. Speaking at Forbes' 30 Under 30 summit, Phan said, *"I thought, if [YouTube] is going to be the global television of the future, I need to build my brand here…Within the first week, 40,000 people watched it and hundreds of comments came in and that's when I realized I'd found my calling."* Just as I have done, and just as I am advising you to do, Phan created a global brand for herself by creating content out of her areas of personal interest and expertise.

Here is a step-by-step guide for signing up for and launching your own YouTube channel:

Step 1: Create a Youtube Account with Google

- If you don't already have a Google account, go ahead and create one!
- Go to YouTube.com, and click the blue "Sign In" button at the upper right hand corner of your screen. Google is now yout "one-stop shop".
- Enter your email — Sign into your Google account.
- You are now registered with Youtube!

Step 2: Set up Your Channel

- Make sure you are signed into YouTube.
- Click the "My Channel" tab on the left side ofyour screen.
- Check to make sure the details are correct, and then confirm to create your new channel.

Step 3: Add Your Personal Brand

- Add a channel description:
- Provide your viewers an overview of what they can expect from your content.
- Use keywords related to your industry or areas of expertise so that users looking for your type of content can find your channel easily.
- You can include links and up to 1000 characters.
- Manage your channel icon:
  - We recommended uploading an 800 x 800 px image.
  - JPG, GIF, BMP or PNG (no animated GIFs).
- Upload channel art using Youtube's preferred dimensions:
  - Minimum width: 2048 x 1152 px.
  - Maximum width: 2560 x 423 px.
  - File size: 4 MB or smaller recommended.
  - learn by consulting the YouTube spec sheet on YouTube.

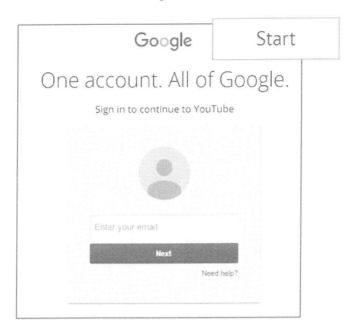

Once you have your account set up, and you're ready to start filming yourself, there are some key points to keep in mind. Make sure to align the style of your videos to the style you have established or are establishing for your brand, and, as we have covered before, make sure that your style is one that you can comfortably live up to and inhabit on a regular basis. Authenticity is compelling; people are drawn to it. And you don't want your video content to ring false to your followers.

Keep your videos short. Viewers have limited attention spans, so the more succinct your video, the more likely it is that they will watch it all the way to the end. According to AdWeek, the ideal length for a YouTube video is around three minutes; as of 2014, the average length of the top fifty videos was two minutes, fifty-four seconds. In addition, viewers have also been trained by YouTube's advertising policies that they have the option to click away from ads after five seconds, so you will want to create video content that doesn't feel like an ad. Instead, offer them meaningful content, whether that is through entertainment or education, such as an instructional video.

Once you start posting content, commit to posting consistently – I suggest posting 1-2 videos per week. As we covered in previous chapters, it is easier to guarantee this consistency if you plan out quality content in advance. Keep it simple. Each video can be focused on one particular tip for your viewers. You can also break up a theme into a series, with each video zeroing in on one step of a process or one aspect of an issue you are explaining. Viral videos may get a lot of press attention, but a disciplined practice of posting quality content on a regular basis can build a large audience over time.

Example of a promotional video posted on YouTube.

Posting consistently yields a number of benefits:

- **You will stay on your followers' radar.** One hundred hours of video are uploaded to YouTube every minute. There is a lot of competition, and you don't want to lose any followers.
- **You will build a content library** that you can draw on and post across other media platforms.
- **Getting regular practice** means that overtime you will get more comfortable on camera, and your videos will get better and better.

Don't forget the "social" element of social media; while your videos themselves may not be interactive, you will have opportunities to engage your followers when they comment on your content. As I encouraged you to do with other social media platforms, take advantage of these opportunities by replying to their comments and posing questions. You can also ask people who watch your videos to subscribe to your channel, either by asking them to click the "subscribe" button in the script of your video, or by using the YouTube feature that allows you to put a call-to-action overlay over your video. When trying to increase your number of subscribers, it doesn't hurt to ask politely for what you want. As on Instagram, you can run contests on YouTube. For example, a while back I asked my subscribers to submit videos of them doing their best Kraig Kleeman impressions, and I got a tremendous response. I had a lot of fun watching the videos, and my followers had a lot of fun making them. Follower submissions mean even more content you can post as the contest goes on, and good-natured contests like this one deepen the connection between your followers and your brand. YouTube also offers free analytics so that you can see which of your videos get the most views and the most engagement in the form of likes or comments. To access the analytics, click on "Video Manager" and then on the "Analytics" tab. Once you know what your audience responds to best, you can focus on particular types of content to drive further engagement. And don't forget to cross-post your videos across your other social media platforms!

ACTION STEPS

Once you're ready to focus on your YouTube channel, answer the following questions in order to reinforce your Winning Brand.

Brand-building Exercise:

- What outfit would you wear for your first video and why?

- Where do you plan to film your first video and why? What advantages or disadvantages do you see in using that space?

- What will be the topic of your first video?

Some Winning Brand Stories

Here are just a few examples of winning brand stories from corporate, sports and entertainment sectors. Note how each of these stories relies on principles we have covered here, such as a clear vision of the brand, drawing on a unique gift mix, memorable tag lines, consistency, authenticity, and engagement with followers.

Warby Parker

Just a few short years ago, the prospect of selling eyeglasses online sounded ludicrous to most people. Eyeglasses were an item people were used to trying on at the eye doctor's office. But Warby Parker, with its winning combination of accessible pricing, retro chic designs, and try-at-home program, became one of the major disruption success stories in recent memory. Before they came along, few people were aware of Luxottica's monopoly on the eyewear industry and its effect on pricing. By bringing this information to light, Warby Parker cofounders Neil Blumenthal, Dave Gilboa, Andy Hunt, and Jeff Raider positioned their brand as being customer friendly and as an alternative to big business. This position is further enhanced by their "buy-one, give-one" policy that, for every pair of glasses sold, pays for the production of a pair of glasses for the nonprofit VisionSpring. In their branding story, they have kept their focus on what they do well. Blumenthal draws comparisons to the simplicity of Apple's products, telling Fast Company, "Apple said, 'We're just going to design a few really well-made, beautiful products and make the process really easy for customers.' I think we looked at it the same way. " Their social media approach reflects their focus on their customers. For example, the nature of their product makes it easy to show people using the product in a variety of settings, so their use of images is strong. In fact, in the summer of 2016, they were using Twitter to promote #seesummerbetter Snapchat filters.

Winning moves: clear brand vision, focus on strengths, consistent social media strategy

Muhammed Ali

Even though Ali enjoyed the heights of his career before the age of social media, I am still including him on this list as a branding success story. I mean, it's hard to think of a better personal moniker than simply "The Greatest," right? That moniker is a distinction that will continue to follow his image and his brand even though he himself is now gone. His Muhammed Ali Center, founded to preserve his legacy, extends his brand by aiming to inspire people to "Be great: Do Great Things." He was a genius at self-promotion. Much like his nickname, "The Greatest," his famous tagline is a perfect example of figuring out your strengths and becoming known for them through a memorable tagline; Ali was known for his quick reflexes and hand speed, and his famous catch phrase "Float like a butterfly, sting like a bee" captures those gifts perfectly. While training, he wore shirts with his own name branded on them. He was also known for his trash talking, a trait he deliberately played up after seeing how much attention the professional wrestler Gorgeous George got from his famously flamboyant antics. According to an article titled "The Branding of Muhammed Ali" that appeared in New Republic shortly after his death, Ali said "[Although] I'd never been shy about talking . . . if I talked even more, there was no telling how much money people would pay to see me." And no one could ever accuse Muhammed Ali of not being bold. As he is famous for saying, "It's not bragging if you can back it up!"

Winning moves: focus on unique gift mix, boldness, memorable moniker and tagline, consistency in brand messaging

Richard Branson

It's impossible to talk about branding success stories without talking about Richard Branson. I started this book by talking about him, so it seems fitting that I circle back to him here. The flamboyant entrepreneur built his empire without adhering to the conventional principles most executives learn in business school, because he didn't go to business school. He achieved his success by figuring out the formula for personal branding. He made himself highly visible, partly by planning outlandish publicity stunts, but also by traveling tirelessly and meeting as many people as possible so that everyone would associate him personally with the businesses he was building. He has always maintained a fierce intellectual curiosity and an awareness of the importance of outside perspectives. In his book Like a Virgin: Secrets They Won't Teach You at Business School, he writes, "bounce every idea you have off numerous people before finally saying, 'We'll give this one a miss,' or, 'Let's do it.'" He has also never strayed from a clear vision of his brand; he describes Virgin as "a fun brand, an adventurous brand, it generally offers great quality at great value, it's a people brand." He reinforces these brand values in interviews and other messaging.

Winning moves: visibility, outside perspectives, consistency in brand messaging

Taylor Swift

I have to pay homage to the millennials among us. When it comes to branding in the digital age, it pays to look at how the millennials are doing it. After all, they are digital natives, so using social media to craft a persona comes more easily to them than for members of previous generations. She may not make my kind of music, but pop star Taylor Swift has cracked the code on fan engagement through social media. She knows her fans follow her on social media, and she communicates with them in ways that set her apart from other celebrities. She and her team selected some of her fans, learned as much as they could about them, and then sent gifts to them, along with a handwritten note from Swift herself. She called the event "Swiftmas." When she released her album "1989," she asked fans to post photos with her album using the hashtag #taylurking (a mashup of Taylor and lurking), and she then retweeted some of the fan photos herself. This is a brilliant move in that it gets fans worldwide to engage with the brand proactively, it cements their loyalty by making them feel special, and the engagement itself provides more content for Swift to post to maintain her brand.

Winning moves: engagement with social media followers, diverse social media content

George Takei

Another celebrity who has mastered the art of social media branding is George Takei. While he already had a considerable fan following from his role as Lieutenant Sulu on Star Trek, his social media presence has exponentially increased his fan base – and has done so decades after leaving the role for which he is most famous. Takei has over 9.8 million "likes" on Facebook, and his "People talking about this" numbers are always remarkably high, which is reflective of high engagement levels. He does repost a lot of his content from other sources (funny videos or memes, etc.), but he is very internet-savvy, and he is careful to choose content that is witty and entertaining to his followers. He also interacts with followers by inviting them to contribute the next meme for him to post. At the same time, he intersperses his humorous content with more serious posts that speak to his role as an activist for LGBT rights or as author of a musical about the experience of Japanese Americans in internment camps during WWII. His good humor and willingness to interact builds a lot of good will with his followers, so that when he does promote something, like his musical or his cologne ("Eau My," named after his sly catchphrase "Oh, myyy"), they receive it positively.

Winning moves: engagement with social media followers, diverse social media content, authenticity

ACTION STEPS

When you think about other strong, winning brands, what comes to mind? What makes those brands stand out in your mind? This exercise will help bring those elements to light.

Brand-building exercise:

- Who are some of your own brand-building heroes, people whose success you would like to emulate, and why?
- Which of the principles in this book can you identify in their success story?
- How can you apply those principles to your own brand journey?

Recap

We've covered a lot of information here, so let's review. To make sure you have a clear step-by-step action plan to build your winning brand in the digital world, I have included a checklist below.

Have you:

- Secured a smart phone with a camera, and/or a laptop?

- Acquired dependable Internet access? Remember, if you don't have Internet at home, you can always use a public library or do work at a local coffee shop or bookstore that offers free Wi-Fi access to customers.

Have you committed to the five winning brand principles? Have you:

- Committed yourself to the right attitude, to being bold, embracing external perspectives, and approaching the process with intellectual curiosity rather than anxiety or judgment?

- Taken inventory of your unique gift mix of talents and skills?

- Decided what sets you apart from others in your field?

- Thought about ways to ensure consistency across your personal brand messaging?

- Expanded your visibility on the digital platforms we've covered here?

For your website, have you:

- Secured a host for your branded website? (Remember, I recommend Godaddy.com.)

- Begun building your website and uploading content?

In determining what makes your brand bold, have you:

- Done a fearless self-evaluation to determine what you want to be known for that is consistent with your talents? Have you asked trusted colleagues, clients, and friends for feedback?

172

- Come up with a memorable personal moniker or tagline?

On Facebook, have you:

- Made a Facebook account, if you didn't have one already?

- Begun posting with intention and fore-thought? In other words, have you stopped posting just anything that comes to mind and started a practice of posting only content that is relevant to your brand and likely to get the attention of your followers?

- Identified a theme (or a few themes) aligned with your personal brand (examples might include family, sports, do-it-yourself projects, fitness, etc.)?

- Clearly defined what goal you hope to accomplish in your use of Facebook, using the SMART goal setting model (Specific, Measurable, Achievable, Realistic, Timely)? Have you aligned your posting strategy to that goal?

- Chosen a profile picture and cover photo that support your personal brand messaging?

- Created a social media calendar to help you remember what to post and when?

- Started to build a diverse content library for your social media calendar so that you are keeping your content fresh, as opposed to only posting photos, for example?

On LinkedIn, have you:

- Created a LinkedIn profile, if you didn't already have one?

- Chosen a recent, professional-looking headshot for your profile?

- Written an accurate headline that reflects your personal brand?

- Made steps toward upgrading your LinkedIn brand, such as posting a video, joining a group and posting in a discussion, or sending invitations to connect?

- Asked someone for a recommendation?

In approaching your overall digital strategy, have you:

- Started getting to know audience by engaging them?
- Experimented with different kinds of content that have different purposes, such as entertaining, inspiring, or informing?
- Stayed true to yourself?
- Established a regular posting schedule for your content?
- Planned out some content in advance?
- Visited online databases such as Pablo by Buffer to collect some images you can use in planning out your content?

On Twitter, have you:

- Made a Twitter account, if you didn't already have one?
- Set a SMART goal for your Twitter activity?
- Selected a profile photo and a header image?
- Defined a clear strategy and social media calendar to plan your posts?

- Increased engagement through actions such as thanking or retweeting your followers or by asking questions?

- Diversified your content to help keep your followers' interest?

- Tweeted @ someone you admire or would like to connect with?

With Hootsuite, have you:

- Signed up and authorized your social media accounts?

On Instagram, have you:

- Made an Instagram account, if you didn't already have one?

- Selected an on-brand profile image and short bio?

- Set your profile to "public" to take advantage of Instagram's organic reach?

- Visited online databases of stock photos – such as Negative Space, Death to the Stock

Image, PicJumbo, or Kaboompics – to select some on-brand images to post?

- Downloaded photo-editing apps – such as Afterlight, VSCO Cam, Snapseed, Camera+, or WordSwag – to help you edit photos and add your own text?

- Thought of a contest you could run for your followers?

For YouTube, have you:

- Created a YouTube account, if you didn't already have one?

- Set up your channel?

- Branded your channel by adding a channel description, channel icon and channel art?

- Acquired a phone with video recording capabilities or a GoPro?

- Decided on your content? In other words, what areas of expertise you will share in your videos?

- Decided on the style and location(s) of your videos?

Next Steps

Now that you've learned about the exact process I used to build my own winning brand, it's time for you to take bold, fearless action. Below are the steps you need to take, beginning right now, to build your brand and establish yourself as one of the best in your industry. Before you know it, you'll have built a loyal following, be seen as the expert in your field, earned more customers, and established a reputation of being the best at what you do.

- Go to my course, A Winning Brand by Kraig Kleeman, which you can access on my site www.kraigkleeman.com, and register. The course will guide you in 20 step-by-step videos and 17 review guides that supplement the content of this book. The course will clarify questions you may have and give you even more in-depth guidance to building your own winning brand.

- Research other brands in your field, and make sure that your participation in the digital world sets you apart from others.

- Continue to track your results so that you will know which approaches work best, and which need fine-tuning.

- Find influencers on each social media outlet and barter with them to have them promote your brand.

- Say "Yes" to any opportunities to partner with larger brands, to speak or vend at events, or to give interviews. Get your brand out there in every way you can, and then use images or video of you at these events to fuel your social media content. Keep giving yourself away until you have so many opportunities that you can start choosing the best ones.

- Take advantage of changes in the season, holidays, and current events to keep your content timely and relevant.

- Remember to experiment with inventive ways to interact with your social media followers.

- Depending on your field, you may want to consider designing a logo for your brand, or hiring a professional to do so.

- Never stop telling your story! Remember, as former Nike executive Scott Bedbury has said, "A brand is a story that is always being told."

Conclusion

He picks up scraps of information —
He's adept at adaptation
'Cause for strangers and arrangers
Constant change is here to stay.
Rush, "Digital Man" – Signals (1982)

Although learning new technologies can be intimidating, it can also be empowering. More importantly, mastering those new technologies is essential for anyone looking to build a brand in today's digital world. As both the real and digital worlds get increasingly crowded, it is becoming more and more crucial to know how to position yourself strategically in today's marketplace. Whether you are a sales professional, an entrepreneur, an artist, a job candidate, or a business owner, this book is designed to give you the tools you need to make yourself visible to the right people in all the right ways. You will of course need to tailor the specifics of web design, color choices, level of formality, etc. to fit your needs and/or the needs of your position or business. But the methods here are sound and will enable you to lay a form groundwork for your brand's social media activity.

If you have gone through all of the review guides and used all of the resources that we have covered, you are on your way to increasing your reach and influence in the digital world. You have secured your own domain, created a LinkedIn profile, started building out your website, started treating Facebook differently than before, started engaging on Twitter and Instagram, started making video content for YouTube, and begun devising your social media posting strategy and schedule. Now, it's time to put it all into practice. As the saying goes, the steps to creating leadership and power are to <u>know</u> it, <u>show</u> it, and <u>grow</u> it! You've read the book, so you now <u>know</u> what actions you need to take. As you have started crafting your social media presence, you are starting to <u>show</u> what you have learned. And the final stage will be when you have mastered your strategies, and you can build on them for continued <u>growth</u>.

As I have discussed, I had zero brand presence just a few short years ago. But I focused on digital assets and outlets, and those efforts paid off exponentially in increased referrals, the ability to command 10x more for my consulting services, over 100,000 social media followers, invitations to speak at star-studded events, and worldwide recognition for my brand. And I spent very little money doing so. I admit that now I sometimes hire videographers, and I use my GoPro for my personal filming, but you don't need any of that to get started. All you need is your phone and access to the internet.

I will close with a story that I hope will continue to inspire and empower you. I was recently in the Philippines working on a client engagement, and one day at lunch several of the women who worked in the company's call center were standing around in the kitchen. One woman exclaimed to the others, "Kaya ko!" and the others responded, equally enthusiastically, "Kaya ko!" As they stood in a circle repeating her words, they all drove their fists into the center of the circle with a lot of energy. I walked over and asked what they were doing, and the one who had spoken first told me that they were getting themselves pumped up for the afternoon. They told me that in their Tagalog dialect, "Kaya ko!" means "I can!" The previous Sunday, their minister had energized all of his congregants by asking them to stand up and declare "Kaya ko!" They found it so inspiring that they adopted it at work. Now I have adopted it, too, and that optimism is the spirit on which I'd like to end this book. We have been on this journey together, and now it is time for you to start establishing your own winning brand. You can!

Work With Kraig

To learn more about Kraig or to find out how you can work with Kraig directly to build your own winning brand, visit www.kraigkleeman.com to join his community, and then register for The Must-React System. Here you can learn about his other services, including:

- Keynote addresses
- Onsite engagement consultations
- Sales Audit Services
- CEO Advisory Services
- Call Center Advisory Services
- Bring The Must-React System Workshop to your business

To contact Kraig directly, send an email to info@kraigkleeman.com or call 877.433.1995.

Be bold, work hard, and be fearless in your quest to develop your brand.

Acknowledgements

This book would not have been possible without the tireless work of both Dana O'Neil and Karissa McCoy. Both individuals assisted me not only with key research and exceptional editing, but they inspired me greatly. Motivation is an awesome thing and I am grateful to both Dana and Karissa for their on-going commitment to excellence and keeping me personally motivated to finish this rich body of work.

One Last Thing

If A Winning Brand has inspired or helped you, I'd love to hear about it!

Email your branding success stories to me personally at info@kraigkleeman.com. Tell me what you did and what gifts or talents you discovered.

Then, help me spread the word. It's harder than ever to stand out in a crowded digital world, but by being bold and fearless, all of our collective hidden talents and gifts can shine. Together, that makes us all stronger.

Give a copy of this book to your friends. Tell others about it, blog about it, make a video about it. Tell others how you've been able to build your winning brand from what you've learned here. And please consider subscribing to my online course entitled "A Winning Brand" by visiting https://awinning brand.com/.

I look forward to personally hearing your stories of your newly discovered winning brand!

Thanks for being bold,

Kraig Kleeman